D1441607

TENDER MURDERERS

WOMEN WHO KILL

By Trina Robbins

Foreword by **Max Allan Collins,**
author of *Road to Perdition*

Cover Illustration: Leslie Cabarga
Cover Design: Leslie Cabarga and Suzanne Albertson
Book Design: Suzanne Albertson
Author Photo: Steve Leialoha

Library of Congress Cataloging-in-Publication Data
Robbins, Trina.
Tender murderers : women who kill / Trina Robbins ;
foreword by Max Allan Collins.
p.   cm.
ISBN 1-57324-821-5 (pbk.)
1. Women murderers. 2. Women murderers—Biography. I. Title.
HV6517.R63 2003
364.15'23'0922—dc21   2002012254

Printed in the Canada.

03 04 05 06 TC 10 9 8 7 6 5 4 3 2 1

Frontispiece

In 1975, artist Becky Wilson drew Carrie Nation, Squeaky Fromme, Bonnie Parker,
Lizzie Borden, and an unidentified victim, for the underground comic book,
Wimmen's Comix. In this book you'll find all the women mentioned, except for
Carrie Nation, who never killed anything bigger than a whiskey bottle.

One
They Did It *for* Love

Two
They Did It *for* Money

Three
Bandit Queens *and* Gun Molls

Four
Fabled Femmes Fatales

Five
Shoots Like a Girl: Women Who Missed

Foreword

Over the past several decades, I've earned a certain reputation as a writer of "true-crime fiction," a contradictory term if there ever was one. That reputation grew out of a number of novels (and short stories and even comics) I've written that combine the traditional hardboiled crime story—what they're calling "noir" these days—with the real people and events who originally inspired the '30s/'40s/'50s "tough-guy" writers like Dashiell Hammett, Craig Rice, Raymond Chandler, Leigh Brackett and Mickey Spillane. (Two of those tough-guy writers are women, by the way—and Mickey isn't one of them.)

The great noir movies and books that have become so accepted in the great American pop-cultural landscape have their own roots in tabloid reality. My distinction, I guess, is that I tend to use the real crimes right down to the real people's names and including details of the events worthy of a nonfiction account. But James M. Cain's *Postman Always Rings Twice* and *Double Indemnity* were derived from the Snyder/Gray murder case; Joseph Lewis's *Gun Crazy*, arguably the greatest of all B-movies, drew from the

Bonnie Parker/Clyde Barrow crime spree (long before the Arthur Penn film); and the Bob Fosse musical *Chicago* had its roots dyed in the Beulah May Annan and Belva Gaertner cases.

And then there's William March's classic horror yarn, *The Bad Seed,* from which blossomed both Broadway and Hollywood productions. March's novel mentions various cases—some real, some imagined—of famous murderers who happened to be female; the ghosts of Lizzie Borden and Belle Gunness loom large in *The Bad Seed's* backstory. March's murderous little girl, Rhoda Penmarck, remains one of the most famous female villains of American literature. My own films, the unofficial *Bad Seed* sequels *Mommy* and *Mommy's Day*—both starring the original Rhoda, the wonderful Patty McCormack—further explore the depths of evil that can hide behind the brittle mask of a beautiful woman's face.

There are those who decry the abundance of black widows and other distaff murderers in noir as evidence of rampant sexism. James M. Cain and Mickey Spillane are perhaps the male authors most commonly criticized for their supposed dark chauvinism. But anyone reading with eyes and mind open will note how remarkable these authors' women are. Cain's murderesses are routinely smarter, more cunning, and better motivated than his thinking-with-the-little-head males. Mike Hammer's secretary, Velda, is as strong and as brave as Mike and even smarter (some would say that's no stretch), and the handful of black widows in Spillane are also strong, well-motivated women.

Is it fair to say that in a culture that relegates women to second place, one option open to a strong woman is to choose a path of crime and even evil? Some of the lethal ladies you are about to meet might be dismissed as weak, but few really qualify for that dismissal. They may be sociopaths, but the women who kill for love and money in these pages are for the most part anything but weak. Sometimes, perversely so, they are admirable.

I have been fascinated with America's female version of Sweeney Todd—Kate Bender—for many years. If you are not familiar with her story, prepare to be spellbound by one of the great waking nightmares; but I would advise sitting with your back close to the wall, and without any snacks in front of you. And who doesn't love Lizzie Borden? Other than her father and mother, I mean.

I take no shame and even a little pride (Kate Bender's inclusion is partly my doing) in reading Trina Robbins's terrific book and knowing that I am a small part of it. There are few things more entertaining than sitting down with a book like this—compact but complete renderings of famous and infamous crimes, titillation and education, going hand in hand!

And now to Trina. First, know that I would love this book even if I didn't already love Trina. Like many of the women you're about to meet, Trina is sweet and deadly. Few genuinely nice people have more spine than this tough-as-nails sweetheart. She used to be a cartoonist (she retired undefeated, a while back) and she is the sort of female artist who could pose for her own pin-up-worthy "pretty girls." I am going to be frank here: Trina is a feminist, and Trina is a babe. I love the fact that she sees nothing at all contradictory about that. Neither do I.

In another time, though—in days even more repressive than these—who knows how Trina's inner strengths might have revealed themselves? Via a bullet, or a sash weight? I can almost see her cutting up a body and stuffing it efficiently into a trunk. All I know at this point is that this is a writer who has skills and weapons I envy: she will lead you through these harrowing pages with precision and yet wry good humor. Trina is the kind of writer who alternates very objective renderings of fact with wonderful outbursts of subjective editorial truth.

I've known Trina for a long time, and I can promise you this: it never takes long to find out what she thinks. And her opinions are doozies, just like the women in this fascinating book. I only hope there is a second volume. There are plenty of crazy dangerous ladies out there, and Trina is just the crazy dangerous lady to tell their stories.

—MAX ALLAN COLLINS

Our interest's on the dangerous edge of things.
The honest thief, the tender murderer. . .

—ROBERT BROWNING, from
Bishop Blougram's Apology

Introduction

As early as 1855, when he wrote these words, the poet Robert Browning echoed a universal fascination with those who willingly cross over the moral line painted by civilization. And of those who knowingly commit the act that separates them from the rest of human society—the taking of another life—woman, "the tender murderer," is the most unusual, and the most fascinating. Despite the fact that we who may have a hard time crushing cockroaches know that murder is the ultimate transgression, we're mesmerized by those rare women, real and fictional, who step where we would never dare, and never wish to.

Killing is something that men do, right? Women stay in their lace-curtained houses, have babies, tend to the vegetable plot out front, and raise their families, don't they? Not always. True, statistics show that 85 percent of all homicides are committed by men, but that leaves 15 percent for the ladies.

What kind of woman takes that step over the edge? What brings her to that point? According to Jean Harris, education has a lot to do with it, with uneducated children more in danger of winding up in prison. Indeed, of the women in this book, Phoolan Devi and Frankie Silver were both illiterate, while Bonnie Parker, Valerie Solanas, and Aileen Wuornos all quit school early to either marry or have a baby. Yet look what happened to overeducated Jean Harris!

Women kill for various reasons. In some cases, love drives them to such a state of desperation that they seem to lose their inborn moral sense. In other cases, it's money, and many women who kill for money are serial killers. Whereas male serial killers act out of twisted sexual urges and usually combine murder with rape and torture, the less than 3 percent of serial killers who are women, like Kate Bender, Belle Gunness, and Dorothea Puente, are more practical. They kill less violently—often with poison—take their victims' money, and neatly bury the bodies in their gardens. Of course, the victims are just as dead.

Many people, when they learned about the book I was writing, brought up the subject of battered women who kill in self-defense. A 1992 study showed that 90 percent of the women in prison for murder had killed the men who abused them. But with the exception of Frankie Silver and Aileen Wuornos, both of whom may have killed in self-defense, I've chosen not to include battered women in this book. Why? *Because we know why they did it!*

In her book, *The Second Sex,* Simone deBeauvoir wrote, "Superiority has been accorded in humanity not to the sex that brings forth but to that which kills." Aha! And when "that which kills" is "that which brings forth"? The result is the runaway popularity of *Thelma and Louise,* a movie that had millions of women weeping because the film's fictional killer heroines had to die for their crime in the end. The result is songs, plays, films, ballets, operas, and even comic books—many bearing little or no resemblance to their subjects—written about real-life and would-be murderesses the likes of Charlotte Corday, Lizzie Borden, Valerie Solanas, Aileen Wuornos, Bonnie Parker, Frankie Silver, and Squeaky Fromme. Whether we're repulsed or sympathetic, we're intrigued by women who kill.

Tender Murderers explores the question of women who kill with a rogue's gallery of twenty fascinating but damned women, from the lyrics of old folk ballads to the pages of yesterday's newspapers. Each of these women, in their time, committed what was then considered the crime of the century, or her trial was the trial of the century. Some of them are ridiculous, some pathetic, some dashing, romantic, and tragic, but they were all notorious. And all of them paid the price for their crimes.

One

They Did It
for Love

Gin and Guns

Beulah May Annan could not have known, when she phoned the police on that afternoon of April 3, 1924, that she would inspire a Broadway play, three movies, and a hit Bob Fosse musical, or that in them her character would be played by the likes of Ginger Rogers and Gwen Verdon. All she could think of at the time was that her lover, Harry Kolstedt, lay slumped against her wall, dying from her gunshot wound, as she told Sgt. John O'Grady at Chicago's Wabash Avenue station, "I've just shot a man!" The startled cop could hear music playing in the background on the other end: it was a jazzy little pop tune called "Hula Lou" ("Who had more sweeties than a dog has fleas").

By the time the cops arrived at Beulah May's apartment they found two men. One was the now very dead Kolstedt, and the other was hubby Albert Annan, who'd arrived after the phone call and tried to take the rap by swearing it was *he* who shot the guy. Beulah wouldn't allow this and went willingly to the police station. Kolstedt "tried to make love to me," she insisted, and she had killed him to protect her honor.

Then she started changing her story. First she admitted that, well yes, she and Harry had been "fooling around" for two months. He came over that afternoon to end their affair, and after sharing what was variously reported as two quarts of moonshine liquor or a half-gallon of wine, she'd shot him rather than give him up. But wait, wait, that's not the way it happened! Actually, she "was the one who was going to quit him." He got mad and—no, no, what really happened was that she had learned about his time in prison. She called him a "jailbird," and he got mad. There was a gun on the bed. He went for it, and she went for it. It was self-defense. And anyway, she was drunk. And anyway, "I fainted."

And all the time this was happening—pick your story—she kept rewinding the phonograph, playing "Hula Lou" over and over.

This is a good time to mention that Beulah May was absolutely gorgeous. A farmer's daughter from Kentucky who'd married and had a baby at sixteen, she had dumped hubby number one and their kid for the fast lane in fabled Prohibition-era Chicago. She was a twenty-three-year-old jazz baby, a sizzling flapper with big blue eyes, bobbed red hair, and the cutest li'l ole southern accent, and she deserved the title she earned: Chicago's Prettiest Woman Killer. While in jail, she acquired admirers—jaildoor Johnnies, who sent her steak dinners and flowers. The newspapers dutifully reported each outfit she wore during her trial: "A simple fawn colored suit with dark brown fur piece that framed the flowerlike face," "slim and straight in her new brown satin crepe frock, with furpiece thrown over one arm," "navy twill tied at the side with a childlike moiré bow—with a new necklace of crystal and jet."

Most of these articles were written by a young journalist for the *Chicago Tribune,* Maurine Watkins. The twenty-eight-year-old Watkins, no slouch in the looks department herself, had just gotten her big break while covering the story of another murderess, a thirtyish divorcee named Belva Gaertner. Like Beulah May, Belva shot her man because he was doing her wrong—leaving her, that is—about a month before Beulah May dispatched Harry Kolstedt. And like her red-haired flapper sister on Chicago's Murderess's Row, her defense was that she was drunk and couldn't remember a thing. "Gin and guns—either one is bad enough," she said, "but together they get you in a dickens of a mess, don't they."

It was Beulah versus Belva, competing for headlines and selling papers. Chicago's newspaper readers were having the time of their lives, and Maurine Watkins was racking up bylines. News photographers posed the two murderesses together for the front page. Belva, a one-time cabaret dancer, was a bit too over-the-hill for the Prettiest Killer title, so Watkins dubbed her The Most Stylish of Murderess's Row, and outdid herself describing her outfits: "A blue twill suit bound with black braid, and white lacy frill down the front; patent leather slippers with shimmering

French heels, chiffon gun metal hose. And the hat—ah, that hat! helmet shaped, with a silver buckle and cockade of ribbon, with one streamer tied jauntily—coquetishly—bewitchingly—under her chin."

The Assistant State's Attorney queried a prospective juror, "Would you let a stylish hat make you find her 'not guilty'?"

Belva's lawyer wisely postponed her trial until after Beulah's. If Beulah got off, so would Belva. And Beulah played her trump card: she was pregnant! "Beulah Annan Awaits Stork, Murder Trial," ran Watkins's headline.

Beulah May had yet another tale for the jury: When a drunken Harry Kolstedt came to her door, she begged him to leave, and "I told him I was going to have a baby." She threatened to send him back to prison if he wouldn't leave her alone, and they both went for the gun. Beulah got the gun, and Kolstedt turned to get his hat and coat, but "didn't get that far."

And why didn't he get that far?

"Darned good reason," testified Beulah May. "I shot him."

On May 25, 1924, a jury of handsome young bachelors found Beulah May not guilty. Less than a month later, Belva Gaertner was also found not guilty. Beulah divorced Albert, the faithful husband who'd stood by her during her trial, and married an ex-prizefighter named Edward Harlib. That lasted about a year, until Beulah discovered that he was already married.

↬ In this artist's interpretation from the 1940s, Beulah phones for help, while her lover slumps over, dead, in the background.

As for Maurine Watkins, she went on to study at the Yale School of Drama, and wrote a play based on the story of Beulah May Annan: *Chicago.* On the stage, Beulah May was given the classier name Roxie Hart, and Belva was re-christened Velma. The play, a satiric comment on media circuses and trials of the century, opened on Broadway in 1926 and was an instant hit, playing for a respectable 172 performances. *Chicago* was turned into a silent movie in 1928, and filmed again in 1942 as *Roxie Hart,* with Ginger Rogers in the title role. Finally it was adapted into the classic Bob Fosse musical, opening on Broadway in 1975. The most recent incarnation of Beulah's story is the 2002 movie, an adaptation of Bob Fosse's musical starring Renee Zellweger as Roxy and Catherine Zeta-Jones as Velma, a.k.a. Belva.

Belva herself, dressed to the teeth, came to the opening of the 1926 play. "Sure, that's me," she said, of Velma.

Beulah May didn't make it to the opening. She'd had a mental breakdown after her third divorce, signed herself into a sanatorium under an assumed name, and died there of tuberculosis, a year later.

⤳⤳⤳ The Movie ⤳⤳⤳

Even though it was filmed in black and white, Ginger Rogers dyed her blonde locks orange for the role of the floozy flapper Roxie Hart in the 1942 film. The movie's snappy dialogue borrowed heavily from the original play, which in turn borrowed heavily from Maurine Watkins's own real-time articles and interviews with the celebrity murderesses. There was one fatal difference: post-code Hollywood simply couldn't make a film in which the killer, male or female, got away with it. Crime Doesn't Pay was the byword of the day. Never mind that fate stepped in for the *real* Roxie to make sure that she *did* eventually pay for her crime; *Roxie Hart* was a comedy that most certainly could not end with the heroine's death in a sanatorium. So the story was changed to make Roxie innocent! In the movie, it's Roxie's husband who shoots his wife's lover, but Roxie, a wannabe hoofer, is persuaded to take the rap because it'll make her famous and be good for her career.

Rent the video, if you can find it, to see Ginger Rogers turn in a topnotch performance as the gum-snapping, wisecracking Roxie, and to see her dance, without benefit of Fred Astaire, a fabulous Black Bottom.

↜ Beautiful Beulah

"Count the Heads!"

This much is agreed upon: On October 16, 1931, pretty, blonde, twenty-six-year-old Winnie Ruth Judd shot to death Anne LeRoi and Hedwig "Sammy" Samuelson, stuffed their bodies (one of which was dismembered) into two trunks and sent them by train to Los Angeles.

The rest of the story depends on whom you want to believe: Winnie or the prosecution.

In 1930, Winnie left her husband of four years and moved to Phoenix, Arizona, for her health. She had tuberculosis, and in those days Phoenix, with its dry hot air, was where you went for the cure. Anyway, her marriage was a shambles: her doctor husband was fat, balding, and twenty-two years older than she, his practice was a flop, and he was addicted to his own drugs. She found work as a medical secretary at a clinic, and took up with "Happy Jack" Halloran, an influential, well-to-do Phoenix businessman, who happened to also be married. She also took up with Anne and Sammy.

Thirty-two-year-old brunette Anne and her roommate,

twenty-four-year-old blonde Sammy, had met in Alaska, and moved to Arizona together because of Sammy's TB. Winnie roomed with them briefly, but after some typical roommate clashes—Winnie was a bit of a slob, the other two were neatniks—she moved into her own bungalow.

Anne and Sammy were what in those days were called "party girls"—possibly also, according to newspaper reports, bisexual party girls and lesbian lovers. (The newspapers delicately called it "strange intimacies." It was even hinted that Winnie might have been part of a lesbian triangle.) Whatever the truth, no one argues over the party girls bit. The girls threw shindigs in their studio duplex for various married Phoenix businessmen, one of whom was Happy Jack. The men would supply bootleg booze, and leave behind wads of dough. We can assume that what was played in that little duplex was more than simple games of Mah Jong. Winnie knew about Happy Jack's relationship with Anne and Sammy, but said nothing. After all, who was she to cast the first stone?

Anyway, she loved Happy Jack. So much, in fact, that she even helped him get girls. Sometime during the week of October 15, 1931, Happy Jack told Winnie that he and his pals planned a deer-hunting trip to the mountains. Winnie introduced him to Lucille Moore, a pretty nurse who worked at her clinic. Lucille came from that part of Arizona, knew the terrain and animals, and would love to come along. Winnie must have guessed what would go on between Happy Jack and Lucille during that hunting trip. At any rate, Anne and Sammy did.

On Friday night, October 16, Happy Jack was supposed to take Winnie out to dinner, but he stood her up. Annoyed, and with nothing else to do, she took the trolley to Anne's and Sammy's duplex, hoping to get in on a game of bridge. By the time she arrived it was getting late, and the roommates suggested she stay over; the trolley would soon stop running for the night, and in the morning she could go to work with Anne, who also worked at the clinic.

It was when they all got to bed (drinking warm milk!) that the fur started flying. Anne started it: How could Winnie have introduced Jack to Lucille? Didn't she know that Lucille had syphilis and would give it to Jack? Anyway, Winnie was a tramp, and what would her husband think if he knew how his wife was carrying on with Happy Jack? Winnie fought back: Oh yeah? Well, *everybody* at the clinic, she said, knew that Anne and Sammy were nothing but lesbo-perverts.

At a certain point, went Winnie's later testimony, she decided she'd had enough, and went to the kitchen to put her empty milk cup into the sink. Hearing a noise behind her, she turned, and there stood Sammy with a gun aimed at her chest. Winnie grabbed a bread knife from the counter, and the two women fought. She stabbed Sammy in the shoulder; Sammy shot her in the hand.

Meanwhile Anne was hitting Winnie over the head with an iron-ing board, yelling for Sammy to "Shoot her!" Winnie got hold of the gun and shot them both dead.

She threw on her dress and shoes and fled. The trolley was still running; she took it home and arrived there around 11:30, to find Happy Jack on her doorstep, drunk as a skunk. Not believ-ing her hysterical report, he drove them back to the duplex to see for himself. She wanted to call the cops. After all, it had been self-defense. No way, Jose, said Happy Jack, he would take care of it, and she mustn't tell a soul.

Winnie mopped the bloody kitchen floor, and Jack dragged a huge trunk in from the garage. She was to go home, he'd take it from there. The next evening, when Winnie met Jack back at the duplex, the bodies had been neatly stashed in the steamer trunk. He admitted that he'd had to "operate on" Sammy a bit, to get her to fit. His plan was to ship Winnie, along with the trunk, to Los Angeles, where he'd have a man meet her and dispose of the bodies. He got her a ticket for the Golden State Limited express train to Los Angeles.

Immediately, everything went wrong. The deliverymen hired to lug the trunk to the train station told her it was too heavy; she'd have to separate the contents into two trunks. Jack had conve-niently disappeared, and Winnie was left with the gruesome task of dumping bits and pieces of Sammy into another trunk. As

Winnie described it, "I didn't lift (the body parts), I lowered them over the edge and they fell into the lower (trunk)."

After distributing the various parts evenly in the two trunks, there remained only Sammy's legs. She stuffed them into her valise. The landlord and his son helped her get the trunks to the train, where she had to pay $4.50 extra because they still weighed too much.

Of course nobody was there to meet Winnie on the station at Los Angeles, and when she phoned Jack she was informed that he was gone on a hunting trip. Meanwhile the two trunks, stinking to high heaven and leaking blood, were opened by suspicious railroad officials. Here's the description from the *Los Angeles Examiner* for October 20:

> In the larger one was the body of an older and larger woman. . . . In the body of (a) younger woman were three bullet wounds. . . . She had been stuffed into the smaller trunk, for the body had been severed by a keen-edged instrument—cut completely into three pieces, but the portion from the waist to the knee was missing!

The missing parts were found that evening, still dressed in the remains of pink pajamas, stuffed into a valise and hidden behind the door of the lady's room in the train station.

The newspapers ate the story up! Almost as soon as news of

≈ Newspaper artists didn't always get it right. This drawing, from a newspaper of the day, incorrectly shows Winnie shooting either Anne or Sammy in bed (the deed was done in the kitchen), and the grisly discovery in the trunk.

the gruesome discovery reached his desk, *Los Angeles Examiner* reporter Warden Woolard was on the phone to Detective Bill White for juicy details. How many bodies were in the trunk, he asked. White answered, "I dunno, it's just one helluva mess." Woolard snapped, "Good God, Bill, can't you count the heads?"

Headlines referred to Winnie first as "The Tiger Woman," and "The Velvet Tigress," then as "The Trunk Murderess." That Sammy's body had been chopped up to fit in the trunk made her crime all the more titillating to the public, despite the fact that, if you think logically about it, chopping Sammy up didn't make her any deader than she already was.

A massive womanhunt finally ended when Winnie was found hiding out in, ironically, a mortuary. And when she was brought to trial, things really heated up. Winnie claimed self-defense. The prosecution said she'd killed the two women while they slept, in a fit of jealousy over their relationship with Happy Jack. As for lover boy himself, the Phoenix high muck-a-mucks protected their buddy as best they could. Although he was named in every other newspaper in America, the Phoenix papers simply referred to him as "Mister X." Neither he nor Winnie were even called to the witness stand. And of course, the lesbian angle was brought up. At one point, the trial psychiatrist, after being told by Winnie that she loved both her husband *and* Happy Jack, asked her if she was polyandrous. She shot back indignantly, "There was nothing between those girls and me!"

On February 8, 1932, poor Winnie was sentenced to be hanged by the neck until dead.

But it didn't end there. The general public, from children who sold magazine subscriptions door to door to help her defense, to First Lady Eleanor Roosevelt, thought Winnie had been railroaded to protect a certain party. The petite, 100-pound woman, they felt, couldn't possibly have managed dismembering the bodies and squeezing them into a trunk all by herself. Eventually, thanks to the combined efforts of Sheriff John R. McFadden and prison warden A. G. Walker, Winnie won a Grand Jury hearing and then a sanity hearing. The sanity hearing opened on April 14, 1933, the day she'd been scheduled for death. She was ruled insane and committed to the Arizona State Mental Hospital for life.

⤜⤜⤜ Winnie, the Escape Artist ⤜⤜⤜

Winnie was an ideal patient at the funny farm, styling the hair and nails of her fellow inmates, and soon even beautifying the nurses, in return for a small payment. The only problem was, she kept escaping. Between 1939 and 1952, she escaped six times, staying out from only a few hours to six days. Finally, in 1962, she escaped a seventh time and remained free for almost seven years. She found work with a rich Oakland, California, family, caring for their aged mother. The family loved her, and when the old woman died (of old age!), they invited Winnie to stay on in a cottage on their property. That's where the police found her when they finally tracked her down through her driver's license.

This time Winnie got world-famous attorney Melvin Belli to handle her defense. He lost his fight to avoid her extradition back to Arizona, but her sentence was finally commuted in 1971. Winnie walked out of the mental hospital a free woman, and returned to California, living quietly in Stockton under an assumed name, with Skeeter, her dog. On October 23, 1998, at the age of ninety-three, she died peacefully in her sleep.

Some things, however, never change. Winnie's obituary in one newspaper was headlined, "Insane Murderess Dies of Old Age."

Integrity Jean and the Diet Doctor

When Dr. Herman Tarnower, author of the bestselling Scarsdale Diet book, was shot and killed by a discarded lover, a large number of American women applauded. Many of them were feminists, who objected to the incessant message pushed by this and other diet books, that women must be slim at all costs. Others were women who had tried the diet.

If you read his book and attempt to follow his diet, you soon get the impression that Dr. Tarnower, or Hi, as his friends called him, may have been a culinary sadist and fascist. It is not a pleasurable diet. One example is the between-meal snack he permits the reader: carrot and celery sticks only, with no substitutions. Of course, it may never have occurred to him that a person could get so sick of carrot and celery sticks that she never wanted to see one again. Or, perhaps it didn't occur to him that raw broccoli, cauliflowerets, or radishes might provide low-calorie snacking and help prevent death from monotony. Or perhaps he felt contemptuous of the women struggling to lose weight by following his directions. At any rate, when one woman wrote to him, begging to substitute cauliflower and radishes for the omnipresent carrots and celery, his answer was the author-itarian, "Stick to the Diet as listed!"

In the days following March 10, 1980, as the facts emerged of Hi's treatment of his dumped lover, and now killer, Jean Harris, it would seem that his sadism and fascism, and his contempt for women, went beyond the pages of his book.

Jean Harris never fit the profile of so many other women who kill: she never grew up with poverty and poor education, she experienced no early marriage or teen pregnancy. Born in 1923 and brought up by well-to-do parents, she attended Smith College and graduated magna cum laude. Married, divorced, mother of two kids, she became a teacher, and by 1977, was headmistress of the Madeira Girls' School, an expensive private girls' high school in Virginia. She had such high moral standards that her nick-name was Integrity Jean. She was twin sets and pearl necklaces, and well-coifed blonde hair. She had class. She was a lady.

But inside, Jean had been unraveling for years. Shortly after her divorce in the mid-1960s, she had met Herman Tarnower, and the two quickly became an item. In 1967, he proposed to Jean, giving her a diamond ring worth $35,000. But within the year, he backed out of their betrothal—he just wasn't the marrying kind, he told her. Jean accepted that they would never marry, and their relationship continued. They traveled to exotic places together: Hawaii, Bali, Singapore. Soon, however, Jean understood something else about Hi: he was sleeping around, he would always have other women in his life. But she loved Hi and was willing to accept that. The other women didn't matter to Jean, as long as she stayed the number one woman in his life.

What all these women saw in Hi Tarnower is beyond me. Born in 1910, he was much older than them, balding, and just plain ugly. In a satiric article written after he was killed, *National Lampoon* magazine described him as looking like a squid. People who knew or had met him described him as charming, but it's hard to imagine Hi's charm being reason enough to go to bed with him.

Nonetheless, Hi was living the life of a medical Hugh Hefner, and in trying to accept his lifestyle Jean was growing depressed—except that she didn't realize she was depressed. She thought she was just tired. In fact, she felt more and more exhausted as their relationship progressed, and the Good Doctor prescribed medicine for her: a drug called Desoxyn. Desoxyn is actually a brand name for methamphetamine—speed. Doctor Hi had been keeping Jean on speed, with a little Valium on the side, since at least 1978.

The biggest cause of Jean's depression was Hi's secretary-receptionist, Lynne Tryforos. Around 1974, Lynne, younger than Jean, became a rival for Hi's affections. Soon, when he traveled with Jean, Hi would leave his itinerary with Lynne. When Jean wasn't spending the night with him, Lynne was. When Jean showed up, Hi would simply move Lynne's things out of the closet. When Lynne came over, he'd hide Jean's things. Nevertheless, once Lynne found Jean's clothes, and slashed them. And during a trip to Paris in 1977, when Jean and Hi returned to their hotel room, Hi left a letter from Lynne on the floor, where Jean could find it, and on the mantel, he left a pair of gold cufflinks, inscribed, "All my love from Lynne."

Did Hi make sure they found each other's possessions? Did he derive a sadistic pleasure from the torment both women must have felt? Did he enjoy being fought over? You bet he did! And they did fight over him. Jean began receiving anonymous phone calls in the middle of the night. In return, she started phoning Lynne and screaming at her. Lynne changed her unlisted phone number five times, but somehow Jean always found it. On New Year's Day 1979, Lynne actually paid for an announcement on the front page of the *New York Times,* reading, "Happy New Year, Hi T. Love always, Lynne." Jean's caustic comment was, "Why don't you suggest she use the Goodyear Blimp next year? I think it's available."

By March 1980, Jean Harris had finally become undone. There was trouble at the Madeira Girls' School: pot paraphernalia, pots seeds and stems, had been found in the possession of four students. "Integrity Jean" insisted on expelling them, even though they were about to graduate. There was a student demonstration protesting her ruling. She received angry letters from the girls' parents, and even a critical letter from a young student whom Jean held in high regard.

Jean grew more and more insecure. The previous year, a professional evaluation group hired by the school had recommended her dismissal. She was not rich, and the strong possibility of being fired was almost more than she could cope with, on top of Lynne shoving Hi's infidelity in her face. Not only that, but she had run out of her prescription "medicine."

The last straw for Jean was a dinner planned by the Westchester County Heart Association for April 19, at which Hi, whose diet book was now number one on the *New York Times* bestseller list, would be the honored guest. He had invited both women to the dinner (why couldn't they see how much he enjoyed playing them against each other?), but neither would sit at the head table with him. Jean would sit with friends, while Lynne got to sit at a table that was closer to Hi. Jean, who had helped Hi by editing his book, found this insufferable. She deserved to sit next to him! She composed a letter to Hi. The letter, which became known as the Scarsdale Letter, clearly shows Jean's rage—she refers to Lynne as "your adulterous slut" and "your whore"—but much more disturbing is the masochism she displays:

> You keep me in control by threatening me with banish-ment—an easy threat which you know I couldn't live with—and so I stay home while you make love to someone who has almost totally destroyed me. {Why couldn't she see that it was Hi who was destroying her?} I have been publicly humil-iated again and again but not on the 19th of April. It is the apex of your career and I believe I have earned the right to watch it—if only from a dark corner near the kitchen.... She has you every single moment in March. For Christ sake give me April. T. S. Eliot said it's the cruelest month—don't let it be, Hi. I want to spend every minute of it with you on weekends. In all these years you never spent my birthday with me. There aren't a lot left—it goes so quickly. I give you my word if you just aren't cruel I won't make you feel wretched.

Of course, she knew that her letter would have no effect on Hi. As far as he was concerned, she was yesterday's news. Jean had bought a .32-caliber revolver in 1978 for protection, although she never learned how to use it properly. Now she contemplated suicide. She felt that she just needed to talk to Hi once more before dying. She phoned and begged to see him. He wasn't inter-ested, finally grudgingly muttering, "Suit yourself."

(At this point, dear reader, are you shouting, "Shoot him, shoot him!"? *I* am.)

She made a will, and left a note for Alice Faulkner, president of the school board:

> I'm sorry. . . . Next time choose a head the board wants and supports. Don't let some poor fool work like hell for two years before she knows she wasn't ever wanted in the first place. There are so many enemies and so few friends.
>
> I was a person no one ever knew.

Then she drove for five hours to Hi's Scarsdale home, with the gun in her purse and a bouquet of flowers on the seat next to her.

What happened next is what the trial was all about. Both sides agree on one thing: Jean Harris did shoot and kill Dr. Herman Tarnower. The prosecution argued that she planned to kill him—if she couldn't have him, no one would—and then kill herself. Jean's version is different.

Arriving at Hi's house at II P.M., seeing all the lights out, she let herself in through the garage and, carrying the flowers, climbed the stairs to Hi's bedroom, waking him up. He wasn't exactly welcoming, grumbling, "Jesus, Jean, it's the middle of the night!"

↜ The famed diet doctor. Was he worth it?

Earlier that evening, Lynne had been one of his dinner guests.

"I've brought you some flowers," she said hopefully.

But Hi didn't want to talk. He closed his eyes and muttered, "Jesus, Jean, shut up and go to bed."

Laying the flowers on the bed, Jean went into the bathroom. Turning on the light, she saw Lynne's things there—her nightgown and curlers—and the rage inside her exploded. She threw the nightgown on the floor, stomped back into the bedroom, and hurled the box of curlers through the window. Hi, who'd leaped out of bed by now, smacked her hard across the face—to snap her out of it, we assume. At any rate, he had never hit her before.

The melodrama increased. Jean said, "Hit me again, Hi. Make it hard enough to kill." When Hi didn't respond, Jean fished the gun out of her handbag, raised it to her head, and pulled the trigger. Hi tried to grab it from her, and the first shot got him in the hand. The gun dropped to the floor, Hi ran to the bathroom to doctor his badly bleeding hand, and Jean retrieved the gun. They wrestled for it again, and this time he received the shot that killed him. As he lay dying, Jean again tried to shoot herself, but the gun just clicked; she had used up the bullets. There were more bullets in her pocket, but Jean didn't know how to reload the gun. She banged it on the bathtub, trying to eject the spent shells, and succeeded in breaking it.

Jean was no professional gunwoman.

Panicked, she ran downstairs, shouted to the servants, "Somebody turn on the goddamn lights! I'm going for help!" she got in her car and headed for the nearest pay phone, only to turn right around again when she saw a police car headed for the house, and give herself up.

Nobody really wanted to send Jean to prison. Members of the jury were crying when they announced that they had found her guilty of murder in the second degree. The judge's voice broke when he gave her the mandatory fifteen years to life sentence.

Before her sentencing, Jean delivered a speech so stirring that it moved the courtroom to applause. But she had already summed it all up in the preliminary hearings, when she had said, "I loved him very much, he slept with every woman he could, and I had it."

~+~+~+~+ Life after (Hi's) Death ~+~+~+~+

Years after she was pardoned by New York Gov. Mario Cuomo, Jean Harris said in a television interview, "What makes prison really horrible is the hours wasted there." But Jean did not waste her time while in prison. In the New York Bedford Hills Correctional facility, Jean soon discovered that 80 percent of women in prison are mothers, and that less than 50 percent of them have completed high school. Their children are terribly at risk. In an article written by Sarah L. Rasmusson for the online magazine, *Women's eNews,* Jean is quoted as saying, "These kids are pushed through the foster care system, the worst schools, and they grow up in the poorest communities. The prison cycle just continues."

So Jean, whose answer to "How did you survive in prison?" was "Perhaps it's the old schoolteacher in me," founded the Children of Bedford Fund, raising money to educate the children of the women with whom she shared a life behind bars for twelve years. She also found the time to write and publish three books while in prison.

Today Jean lives quietly in a small house near the Connecticut River. When she isn't reading and gardening, she lectures on behalf of imprisoned women and their children, and continues to raise money for the Children of Bedford Fund. She says, "It is no coincidence that most people in jail and prison are poorly educated. Keeping kids in school is one of the easiest ways to keep them out of prison."

Ironically, that didn't work for Jean.

"I Would Kill Again"

Aileen Wuornos is the poster girl for women who kill. With a father who was killed in prison, where he was serving time for child molestation, and a fifteen-year-old mother who dumped Aileen and her brother Keith, with their grandparents, she seemed headed from infancy for her final destination, Death Row in Florida's Broward County Correctional Institution. Wait, there's more! Until Aileen was twelve years old, she believed that her grandparents were actually her parents. She had a baby at the age of fourteen, gave it up for adoption, and, when her grandmother died, leaving Aileen and Keith alone with their hard-drinking, overly strict grandfather, she left home, taking to the road and a life of prostitution. Her brief marriage to a much older, well-off man ended when he took out a restraining order on her, accusing her of beating him and blowing his money. With the $10,000 she inherited in 1976, when brother Keith died of throat cancer, she bought a new car and promptly wrecked it. Then she was back on the road.

She collected arrests for petty crimes—drunk driving, assault, disorderly conduct, passing bad checks—the way some women collect shoes. She also collected aliases: Sandra Kretsch, Lori Grody, Susan Blahovec, Cammie Marsh Green.

Aileen's life couldn't have been harder. In a May 4, 2000, interview on the cable network Court TV, she spoke of being homeless from the time she was sixteen, of being raped, held hostage, kidnapped, and tied to beds. She described one man, whom she suspected of being an undercover cop, parking his truck in the woods and taking out a rifle, saying, "Let me screw you with this first." Despite the spate of movies like *Pretty Woman,* which glamorize prostitution, Aileen's experiences were typical for women who sell their bodies. A study of one group of prostitutes showed that they had been raped about thirty-three times in a year.

The situation brightened for a while in 1986 when Aileen met Tyria Moore at a gay bar in Daytona, Florida. The two became a couple; they moved in together, setting up housekeeping in a series of cheap motel rooms. Tyria quit her job as a motel maid and Aileen supported her by prostitution, hitching rides with truck drivers on Florida's interstate highways, charging $30 to $40 for sex. It wasn't much of a life, but Aileen loved Tyria, and made what she considered decent money, at least for a while. But by the end of the 1980s, things headed downhill again. Aileen, never a raving beauty, wasn't doing too good. Fifteen years of hardscrabble existence was reflected on her face, and it wasn't easy supporting Tyria in the manner to which she was accustomed. To make matters worse, Tyria was blowing Aileen's hard-earned money on booze, spending over $100 a night in bars.

Then, in early December 1989, along came fifty-one-year-old electrician Richard Mallory in his 1977 Cadillac. Mallory was bad news; he'd already served ten years for violent rape in Maryland. He picked up Aileen and started bragging, as she related in her television interview, that he wanted to "get some tittie [topless] dancers, get them on video doing some dirty stuff, and then kill them and sell the video." It was the last straw for Aileen, who, for all her life, had been "so ripped apart." She said, "I got so filthy sick of him talking like that, that's what snapped in my head."

Aileen had, understandably, been carrying a .22-caliber gun for self-defense. She shot him three times, and drove the Caddy home to Tyria, explaining where it came from. Tyria didn't want hear about it.

Mallory's decomposed body was found on December 13 near Interstate 95. Soon the bodies of other men were turning up: David Spears, shot six times; Charles Carskaddon, with nine slugs in his body; Troy Burress, with two bullets from a .22; Dick Humphreys, shot seven times; Walter Antonio, with four bullets in his body. Meanwhile, Aileen was coming home with all sorts of tokens of affection for her sweetie—jewelry, cameras, wallets—

and Tyria made it clear that she didn't want to know where any of it had come from.

A seventh man, Peter Siems, went missing on June 7, 1990. His body never did turn up, but his car did, with Aileen and Tyria in the front seats. They wrecked and abandoned it on the following July 4, and this time a witness was able to describe them to the law. Aileen had hurt herself in the crash and left a bloody palm print in the car.

Florida newspapers carried police sketches of the two women, and soon Florida police were on the trail of Tyria and Susan Blahovec/Cammie Marsh Green/Lori Grody/Aileen Wuornos. They caught up with her at a Port Orange biker bar called, ironically, The Last Resort. Aileen was in a bad way. She and Tyria had split up, and Tyria had gone to stay with her sister in Pennsylvania. Aileen, broken-hearted, was drinking heavily, crashing for the night on an old car seat in back of the bar. The cops arrested her on outstanding warrants in the name of Lori Grody; they didn't have enough evidence yet to pin the murders on her. For that, they needed Tyria's help.

They found Tyria at her sister's and convinced her to get Aileen to confess. They flew her back to Daytona, where they put her up in a motel. She phoned Aileen in prison—the calls were taped— saying that she was afraid the cops were about to pin the murders on her. At first, Aileen reassured her, "It isn't us, see? It's a case of mistaken identity." But Tyria phoned back for three days in a row, each call more panicky. Finally, Aileen told her, "I'm not going to let you go to jail. Listen, if I have to confess, I will."

And confess she did, on January 16, 1991. But, she claimed, it was self-defense. In all seven cases. Richard Mallory had raped her, tortured her, sodomized her. Not so the others, though. They had not exactly raped her, she said, but "only began to start to." A jury didn't believe her, and sentenced her to death. Richard Mallory's previous stint in prison for rape was never once brought up during the trial.

It seems very possible, even probable, that Mallory did rape Aileen, or at least threaten her by the things he told her, to the point where she thought he *might* rape her. She'd been raped before. It also seems possible,

↜ *True Crime* comics incorrectly identifies Aileen Wuornos as "the first female serial killer."

even probable, that once she'd killed her first man, Aileen's dammed-up rage came pouring out, and she found it easy to kill the others. In her television interview, she said, "I know I'd kill again, because of the dirt I've been through."

During Aileen's trial, a born-again Christian named Arlene Pralle read about her in the newspaper and started corresponding with her. Jesus had told her to write, she said. Soon Pralle was defending Aileen on talk shows, testifying to the killer's true nature of goodness; she got Aileen interviews with sympathetic journalists, even legally adopted her.

After ten years on Death Row, Aileen, converted by Pralle, changed her tune. She had lied about the self-defense. She'd accepted Jesus, she said, and now had to tell the truth. Newspaper headlines read, "Female Serial Killer Wants To Drop Appeals," and "Prostitute Killed 6 Men Because She 'Wanted To.'"

Perhaps, though, Aileen, tired of ten years on Death Row, just wanted to end it all. Perhaps it wasn't as simple as black or white. Perhaps the truth was closer to what she'd said a year earlier, "When Richard Mallory told me he did time for rape, that made me snap."

When was Aileen lying, and when was she telling the truth? We may never know.

✦✦✦✦ Life after Death Row ✦✦✦✦

Aileen Wuornos is popularly known as America's first female serial killer, but if you read this book, you'll know that isn't true. From Kate Bender in the 1870s, and Belle Gunness in 1908, to Dorothea Puente only ten years before Aileen, women seem to have been quietly doing away with people— mostly men—and burying them in their gardens. What fascinates people about Aileen, though, is the particularly violent, almost *male,* way that she killed her victims. Perhaps it is this reason that she has inspired not only the usual made-for-TV movie and a well-regarded documentary, but a comic, a trading card, and even an opera. *Wuornos,* the opera, composed by Carla Lucero, one of the very few women who have ever written operas, opened in San Francisco on June 22, 2001.

AILEEN WUORNOS

✦ In 1992, Aileen rated her own *True Crime* trading card.

As of this writing, Wuornos, the woman, still waits on Death Row, planning her last meal. In Florida, condemned people are given a choice of the electric chair or lethal injection. Aileen chose the needle.

Two

They Did It
for Money

Indiana Ogress

Female serial killers are comparatively rare, and when they do kill, it's usually for very different reasons than do male mass murderers. Men seem to derive sexual pleasure from their deeds, often combining murder with rape of both sexes. Women, on the other hand, are practical. When they kill more than one person, they do it for money.

Belle Gunness was *very* practical. Perhaps it was because she was born poor. Brynhild Paulsdatter Storset, born in 1859 in Norway, had to work for nearby farmers as a dairymaid while still a girl. Her big sister Nellie emigrated to America in search of a better life, found a husband in Chicago, and in 1883, sent for Brynhild. It was in Chicago that Brynhild met and married Mads Sorenson, a good, hardworking Scandinavian boy. Mads and Brynhild, who now Americanized her name to Belle, opened a confectioner's shop in 1896. The business didn't do too well, and a year later it burned down. Luckily, the couple had insurance. They bought several houses, each of which also burned down. Luckily, they were insured.

Two of their babies died—of acute colitis, said the doctors. They had been insured. And then in 1900, Mads died from what the doctors decided was a heart attack. Belle collected on his two insurance policies totaling $8,000. Poor Belle, murmured her neighbors, she has such an unhappy life!

Belle took the money and her remaining kids, including a foster daughter, Jennie Olson, and bought a two-story brick farmhouse in LaPorte, Indiana, a town with a large Scandinavian population. The house itself had already acquired a shady past; it had been a brothel until the madame died of old age. Belle's new neighbors were no doubt happy to see a respectable Norwegian widow take over the place. Belle put up white lace curtains and fenced in an area behind the building for a pigpen.

By 1902, Belle was married again, to a farmer named Peter Gunness. Peter, a widower, brought along a baby who died a week after the wedding. Belle seemed to lose children the way some of us lose car keys. Peter lasted about a year, before a heavy iron sausage grinder fell onto his head from a top shelf. Daughter Myrtle confided to a school chum that Mama had conked Papa on the noggin and killed him, but nobody paid any attention to what kids say. Belle collected on Peter's $3,000 insurance policy, and dressed herself in black.

But not for long.

Soon Belle was placing ads in Scandinavian newspapers across the Midwest, seeking a husband. "Widow with large farm looking for a helpmate," the ads went, adding that it was important that the prospective groom produce money of his own, so that she would know he wasn't merely a cad after her fortune. She added, "Triflers need not apply." Corresponding with hopeful suitors, she would ask them to bring with them a sum of at least $1,000, to prove their sincerity. In one letter she wrote,

> My dear, do not say anything about coming here. . . . Now sell all that you can get cash for, and if you have much left you can easily bring it with you whereas we will soon sell it here and get a good price for everything. Leave neither money or stock up there but make yourself practically free from Dakota so you will have nothing more to bother with up there.

Standing five feet nine inches high and tipping the scales at 280 pounds, Belle was a true Valkyrie, fit to wear a horned helmet on her blonde head, and she attracted hearty Norse farmers who liked some meat on their women's bones. Ole Busberg of Iola, Wisconsin, traveled to LaPorte to woo her. So did Olaf Lindbloom, Herman Konitzer, Emil Tell, Olaf Jensen, Charles Nieberg, Tonnes Lien, and who knows how many other Olafs, Oles, and Erics. Trouble was, none of them stayed. Belle would be seen with them around town for a few days, hanging on their arm and adding their money to her bank account, then suddenly they'd be gone. Gone back to Minnesota, gone back to Sweden, Belle would say, plowing her fields while wearing the coat and hat they'd left behind, and bemoaning her lot: a poor widow, deserted by another scoundrel who loved her and dumped her. And another ad would appear in the Lonely Hearts section of the *Skandinavian News.*

Somewhere along the way, Jennie Olson disappeared, too. Gone to an exclusive girls' finishing school in California, Belle told the neighbors.

Finally, in January 1908, Andrew Helgelein, a big, good-natured Swede from South Dakota, showed up in LaPorte, bringing with him $1,000 as proof of his good intentions. He and Belle had corresponded for six months, and she had even included a four-leaf clover in one of her letters, for good luck, she wrote. Helgelein had the "good luck" to disappear, like the others. But he left behind a brother, Asa, who, when he hadn't heard from Andrew for some months, wrote to Belle. Belle wrote back: Andrew had returned to the Old Country. Asa didn't buy it. Why would his brother liquidate his property and bring the money to his prospective bride, then suddenly leave her? He announced that he was coming to LaPorte to see for himself.

On April 27, 1908, Belle visited a lawyer. A farmhand whom she had fired, Ray Lamphere, was harassing her, she said, and just in case anything happened to her, she wanted to make a will, leaving her money to her children. If they didn't survive her, the will stipulated that the money would go to the Scandinavian orphan's home.

In the early morning hours of April 28, Belle's farmhouse burned to the ground. Found in the ashes were the burned bodies of Belle and her three children. Ray Lamphere, the disgruntled farmhand (and also Belle's sometime lover) was dragged out of bed and arrested for arson and murder, protesting all the way. LaPorte looked forward to an exciting trial and a speedy hanging.

There was one problem: the body presumed to be Belle's was missing its head. There were no tests for DNA in those days, but even without the head, it was obvious that this corpse was much smaller and lighter than the hefty widow. The plot thickened: Asa Helgelein showed up in town, suspecting foul play in his brother's disappearance and asking permission to dig around the farm.

Asa's suspicions proved to be dead on, as it were, and on May 5, the first body was uncovered. It was brother Andrew, with fatal doses of arsenic and strychnine in his stomach.

Quickly, the digging crew uncovered more bodies, including that of Belle's teenaged stepdaughter, Jennie Olson, not in the California finishing school after all. Instead she'd been finished right there in LaPorte, possibly because she had grown suspicious of Mama. All in all, at least thirteen bodies were dug up, but the final estimate was higher than that, perhaps forty, because of the numerous bone fragments found in the pigpen. Belle had been feeding her suitors to the pigs.

Ray Lamphere was found guilty only of arson, because it was impossible to prove whether or not the headless corpse was Belle. He was sent to prison for two to twenty years, and died there of tuberculosis two years later, still insisting that Belle was alive somewhere.

He wasn't the only one who believed she was alive. Sightings of Belle became as common as UFO sightings would be seventy years later. As early as April 29, 1908, a railroad conductor swore Belle had been carried onto his train on a stretcher. On April 30, a local farmer saw her drinking coffee with her best friend. Two boys saw her on April 30 too, and they recognized

✢ Belle, posing as a loving mom, with her doomed kids

her face when she pulled her veil up to drink water from a pump. On July 9, a neighbor spied her walking in her orchard, heavily veiled. His daughters saw her in the woods behind the burned-out house. In 1917, a neighbor recognized her as a patient in the hospital where he worked. In 1931, it was thought that she might be a suspected murderer arrested in Los Angeles; in 1935, a brothel madame in Ohio.

The infamous Black Widow of the heartland lives on today as a beer brewed by LaPorte's Back Road Brewery: Belle Gunness Stout. The brewery describes it as "A notorious drink that is as dark as its namesake's history! A true dark beer lover would die to try it, but it won't kill you."

ᚨᚨᚨᚨᚨ The Ballad ᚨᚨᚨᚨᚨ

Back in the Middle Ages when most people were illiterate, ballads served as the local newspaper, or a musical CNN. Songs about the doings of kings, queens, and bandits, and the latest sensational murder were sung in the market place. Broadsides of the ballad, printed by woodcut, would be sold to the few people who could read. Everyone loves a good scandal, and the songs about murders were some of the most popular. It was centuries before these lyrics were finally written down and published in books or collections, and by then the names of their long-ago composers had long since vanished.

The ballad tradition survived through the centuries and was brought from Europe to the new land: People living in isolated cabins in the mountains or prairies, without access to newspapers, continued to report shocking local crimes in song. Probably the most famous American murder immortalized in ballad form is "Frankie and Johnny," the song about a woman who shot her man because "he done her wrong." The ballad of Belle Gunness is another example.

BELLE GUNNESS

Belle Gunness was a lady fair,
In Indiana State.
She weighed about three hundred pounds,
And that is quite some weight.

That she was stronger than a man
Her neighbors all did own;
She butchered hogs right easily,
And did it all alone.

But hogs were just a sideline
She indulged in now and then;
Her favorite occupation
Was a-butchering of men.

There's red upon the Hoosier moon
For Belle was strong and full of doom;
And think of all those Norska men
Who'll never see St. Paul again.

The Family That Slays Together

The Bloody Benders, America's first serial killers, were descendants of Sweeney Todd and of all the fairytale ogres that haunt children's nightmares. Looking back at their history, it's surprising that this family of German immigrants managed to get away with their crimes over a period of three years. Surely, someone must have noticed all the travelers who checked into the Benders' wayside inn but never checked out.

Yet get away with it they did. Ma and Pa Bender appeared to be a nice old couple, and if their feeble-minded son John made folks nervous, their fears were soon lulled by the appearance of daughter Kate. Kate is reputed to have been a knockout, with a curvaceous figure and long golden hair, and she even had a reputation as a healer and psychic. She ran a small traveling spiritualist show, which she took around to the little towns around their home in Mound Valley, Kansas, and as "Professor Miss Kate

Bender" gave public séances. Her advertisements promised that she could "heal disease, cure blindness, fits and deafness."

But that's not how the money rolled in. In 1871, the Benders had moved into a small one-room cottage located on a main road, about halfway between the small villages of Galesburg and Thayer in Neosho County, Kansas. A canvas curtain divided their single interior room into two rooms. The front room was a restaurant and inn, where weary voyagers could stop for a meal or stay for the night. The back room contained beds for the Bender family, a trap door leading to a stone-walled cellar, and a couple of sledgehammers.

The Benders' hotel was actually a Bates Motel. One of the family—probably not mentally challenged brother John—would hang around outside and strike up conversations with passing travelers, if they were alone and if they appeared to have money. It's a long way to the next town, the Bender would say. Why not stop here to eat, even spend the night? Our rates are reasonable, and Ma Bender cooks up a good German dinner. If the guy had trouble deciding, a come-hither glance from blonde Kate probably helped.

The unsuspecting guest would be seated with his back to the canvas curtain. In all probability, the Benders, being frugal people, didn't believe in wasting a perfectly good dinner, so the hungry guest probably never did get his food. Instead, while he innocently awaited dinner, a hand, probably John's, clutching a sledgehammer, would emerge from behind the curtain and bash in his skull. If that didn't do the job, Kate would reportedly dispatch him by slitting his throat. Then he'd be stripped of money, jewelry, and anything salable, and through the trap door and into the cellar he'd go, to be buried in the orchard behind the house in the dead of night.

If passing travelers turned scarce, Kate, the "mentalist," would add to the family income by bringing in gullible customers for private séances. Following the family scenario, she'd sit them with their backs to the canvas curtain. If her promise was to reunite them with deceased loved ones, she kept her word. One blow from John's sledgehammer, and they joined the dead.

Amazingly, nobody seems to have come looking for a missing son, brother, or husband, until March 1873 when Col. A. M. York showed up on the trail of his brother, who had disappeared while returning from a visit. He'd told York that he'd be stopping at the Benders' inn on his way. Had the Benders perhaps seen him?

No, never, replied the family. Maybe he'd fallen victim to hostile Indians. But wouldn't Col. York like to spend the night?

Their mistake was in not killing him then and there, but perhaps the Benders wanted York to feel more secure before they dispatched him, or perhaps they planned to do him in while he slept. At any rate, that night, alone in the bedroom, York saw something glittering beneath his bed. He pulled it out and held it up: it was a familiar-looking gold locket. Opening it, he saw the faces of his sister-in-law and niece inside; it was his brother's locket!

York slipped out of the house, intending to reach the safety of the nearest town, but on his way to the road he saw lantern light glimmering in the orchard. Hiding behind bushes, he watched Pa Bender and John digging a deep hole in the ground.

Without waiting around to see more, York fled, returning the next morning with a posse of angry villagers. But the house was empty. Perhaps realizing the jig was up when their intended victim escaped, the Benders had skipped town. The remains of at least a dozen

Kate Bender was reputed to be a beauty, but you'd never know it from this nineteenth-century drawing.

people, including York's brother, were found beneath the ground in the orchard.

As for the Benders, they were never seen again, although there were rumors a-plenty. Some said furious vigilantes pursued the family, found them, and lynched them. Some said they went back to Germany to carry on their gruesome trade overseas. As for their little house of horrors, by 1886, a newspaper, the *Topeka Daily Capital,* reported that souvenir hunters had carried off every last stick, including even the stones that lined the bloody cellar.

Today nothing is left, except for the beautiful but deadly ghost of Kate Bender, whom locals say is doomed to walk the land for-ever as punishment for her crimes.

ʌ~ʌ~ʌ~ Was Sweeney Inspiration? ʌ~ʌ~ʌ~

Some of the methods used by the Bender family in dispatching their victims bore a close resemblance to the methods of a cer-tain Sweeney Todd. In the 1780s, Sweeney had a barbershop on London's Fleet Street, right next door to St. Dunstan's Church. His shop was a simple one-room affair, with a single barber chair located in the middle of the floor. But Sweeney had rigged up an ingenious device: the chair was connected to a trap door beneath it, and when Sweeney had a wealthy customer and the coast was clear, he'd pull a lever that sent customer and chair dropping through the trap door into his basement. At the same time, another barber chair would pop up to take the place of the one in the cellar, so that at no time at all was the shop without a chair.

Meanwhile, Sweeney would run hell-bent-for-leather down to the basement. If the fall hadn't killed his victim, Sweeney would help him along into the next world by slitting his throat. Then he'd strip the corpse, taking everything valuable, and expertly carve up the body like a butcher. The human flesh would be delivered to his accomplice and lover, Mrs. Margery Lovett, who ran a meat pie shop on Bell Lane. Mrs. Lovett had a reputation for selling the best meat pies in all of London, and customers would crowd the little store when tempting odors announced a new batch was on its way from the oven.

As for the parts that weren't worthy of pies, the bones, skin, and heads, Sweeney had discovered a tunnel and catacombs beneath the church, and there, among the burial vaults of long-dead parishioners, he distributed the grisly remains of his victims. Sweeney met his downfall when the parishioners of St. Dunstan's began to notice a foul odor coming from below. A search of the tunnels revealed the ghastly rotting remains, and bloody footprints led to Sweeney's barbershop and Mrs. Lovett's pie place. When her customers realized what she had been feeding them, they tried to lynch her then and there, but the London police managed to save her, and Sweeney, for the gallows.

After their executions, Sweeney and Mrs. Lovett were immortalized in cheap magazines of the period, called "penny dreadfuls," and in true crime books and plays, long before Stephen Sondheim produced his famous musical about the barber from hell and his lady accomplice. It's quite possible that old man Bender had read one of these stories, and that a light bulb of inspiration had lit up over his head: if it was a good enough living for the Demon Barber of Fleet Street, it could be good enough for the Bloody Benders.

Dubious Distinctions

Besides having the dubious distinction of being the first woman to be executed in the electric chair in New York State, Ruth Snyder also deserves the title of Most Inept Murderess. When she and her little bespectacled lover Judd Gray killed her husband for his $100,000 insurance, they failed miserably in their attempt to pin the murder on an "Italian looking" stranger, and almost immediately confessed, each blaming the other.

Young Ruth Brown, forced by poverty at the age of thirteen to work as a telephone operator on the night shift, dreamed of becoming secretary to a rich and handsome man, marrying him, and living happily ever after. When she turned twenty her dream came true—sort of. She married her boss, Albert Snyder, the editor of *Motor Boating* magazine, but the happily-ever-after part didn't turn out the way she'd planned. For one thing, Albert had been engaged for ten years to a woman who had died, Jessie Guishard, and he'd never really gotten over her. One of the first things he did when they moved into their new home in Queens, New York, was to put up a picture of Jessie, explaining to his new bride that Jessie was "the finest woman I have ever met." Then he named his new boat after her.

Plus, Albert was boring. Ruth was young, blonde, and pretty, and she had money now. She wanted to enjoy herself, dancing and partying till the wee hours. Albert, whom Ruth started calling "the old crab," preferred to stay at home with their daughter, Lorraine.

It had to happen: in 1925 Ruth met thirty-three-year-old Judd Gray, a quiet little guy with glasses, who worked for the Bien Jolie Corset Company. On their second date, he gave her a corset, fitting it himself behind locked doors in the privacy of his office. They started meeting for afternoon quickies at the Waldorf. Ruth would bring little Lorraine with her, and the kid would play in the lobby while her mother and Judd Gray were otherwise occupied. He called her Mommie. The tabloids would call her The Iron Widow and The Bloody Blonde. Oh, and by the way, Gray was married.

During 1926, Ruth was already toying with murder, and Albert had some close calls. Judd Gray testified that Ruth had tried poisoning her husband with dichloride of mercury "when he had hiccoughs," and had twice fed him knockout drops and turned on the gas. She even tried out sleeping powders on Gray himself, to see if they worked. But Albert stayed alive. Ruth told Gray, "I don't have any luck," and started hinting broadly that they needed to do something more. Perhaps, she suggested, Albert "might be drowned that summer."

Instead, on March 20, 1927, they chloroformed him, tied him up, smashed in his head with a sash weight, and strangled him with wire. Ruth made sure that Judd Gray tied her up, too, so she could blame it on a burglary, and when her daughter fetched the neighbors, she wouldn't let them untie her. She needed the law to see her bound.

Their carefully woven plans unraveled almost immediately. Ruth told the police that her jewels were missing, but she'd been too greedy to actually part with them, so the cops found them hidden in her mattress. They also found the bloody sash weight, a tie clip with Judd's initials, and his name in her little black book.

'Murder Will Out'

SLAIN IN SLEEP   GUILTY LOVERS

↬ A newspaper artist's rendition of the Snyder murder shows Albert Snyder calmly dead in his bed. In reality, with his head caved in with a sash weight, he didn't look that good.

And they found Judd hiding out in upstate New York. He had left a trail a mile wide, first asking directions of a cop at the bus stop, then taking a taxi into Manhattan. The taxi driver remembered him because cheapskate Judd had tipped him a whole nickel.

Love flies out the window when the cops beat down the door, and immediately each accused the other of being the one respon-

+~+ Ruth, as drawn by Nell Brinkley *(left)* and Fay King *(right)*

sible. He forced me to go along with it, insisted Ruth. I was "her love slave," completely under her influence, swore Judd.

The trial was a media circus, and the newspapers had a field day. They printed photos of socialites shoving their way into the courtroom. Popular writer Damon Runyon covered the trial, and described Ruth: "A chilly-looking blonde with frosty eyes and one of those marble you-bet-you-will chins." The Hearst papers had two women cartoonist/columnists, Fay King and Nell Brinkley, who took turns covering the trial, then reporting the "women's angle" in the dailies, complete with illustrations. Fay King wondered "if [Ruth Snyder's] life would have been different if bobbed hair and flapper styles had not been so becoming to her?" Sob sister Nell Brinkley reported that Ruth's "mother had come to her side—a dear old lady, as quiet as a mouse. She has rallied to her daughter's aid." Brinkley, who was famous for the pretty girls she drew, glamorized Ruth in the portraits she did of her, but Fay King, not as kind, drew Ruth with the "marble you-bet-you-will chin" that Damon Runyon had described. After drawing Ruth until their hands got tired, King and Brinkley switched to Judd Gray's wife and the mothers of both defendants. Poor Gray was largely ignored.

He turned to religion, and sat quietly during the trial, glumly accepting his fate. Ruth's attitude was more of a "What, me worry?" She had received 164 proposals of marriage while in prison, and she was confident that she'd escape The Chair. "They will never send a woman to the death house in this state," she said.

Woops, wrong again, Ruth! The couple were found guilty on May 9, 1927, and sentenced to death. They were electrocuted, Ruth first, and then Judd, on January 22, 1928. She was such a bungler that you can almost feel sorry for her.

↜↜↜↜ The Picture ↜↜↜↜

Ruth and Judd's sordid story inspired the noir 1944 film *Double Indemnity,* with Barbara Stanwyck as a suitably brassy 1940s version of the deadly flapper.

And then there was The Picture. One of the official witnesses at Ruth Snyder's execution was a young *New York Daily News* photographer named Thomas Howard. He had smuggled in a camera, taped to his leg. When the current went on, his camera went off: he crossed his legs, uncovering the camera, squeezed a bulb hidden in his pocket, and snapped the picture.

The next day the picture, now considered one of the most famous photos in the history of photojournalism, occupied the entire front page of the *New York Daily News.* Ruth sold one million extra copies for the *Daily News* that day and earned a third dubious distinction: Cover girl at the moment of her death.

⌇ The Picture

Arsenic and Old Lace Redux

In the 1940s dark comedy *Arsenic and Old Lace,* the sweetly homicidal maiden-lady Brewster sisters take in lonely old men and, wanting to put them out of their misery, dose them with arsenic-laced elderberry wine and bury them in their basement. In a case of life imitating art, kindly, white-haired Dorothea Puente took lonely old people—often alcoholic, drug addicted, or mentally ill old people—into her boarding house, put them out of their misery with cocktails of potentially lethal drugs and alcohol, buried them in her garden, and cashed their Social Security checks.

Everyone loved the sweet widow lady who ran her boarding house in a blue-and-white gingerbread building. The retired doctor, who still called herself Dr. Puente, played auntie to so many needy young people, gave to so many charities, opened her house to the neighborhood on Christmas and Easter. A lady all the way, she was always impeccably dressed and perfumed, wearing real jewelry, and she had such fascinating stories to tell about her experience as an army nurse on the Bataan Death March. Wasn't it sad that she had cancer? And everyone agreed that seventy-year-old Dorothea, born in Mexico into a family of eight children, was a wonderful cook!

Not. To start with, she wasn't Mexican (she wasn't a doctor, either). And she was never widowed. Born Dorothea Helen Gray, in 1929—she was also a good ten years younger than she let on—in San Bernardino, California, to a physically and mentally ill father and an alcoholic mother, she was orphaned by the age of six. Raised by relatives, Dorothea had to work at picking fruits and vegetables while still a child. At an early age she started making things up, perhaps in an attempt to deny the reality of her wretched life. In high school, she told her classmates that she was a Portuguese exchange student. She married at seventeen, using the name Sherriale A. Riscile. The marriage lasted three years, and Dorothea—she was not widowed—entered a life of crime before she was even twenty, serving four months in jail for writing bad checks. Her second marriage, at the age of twenty-three, was to Axel Bert Johanson. This time she called herself Teya Singoalla Neyaarda (where did she get those names?) and claimed to be an Israeli-Egyptian Muslim. That marriage lasted fourteen years, but Johanson, a merchant seaman, was often away for months at a time, and during his absences Dorothea seems to have consoled herself with a long list of men. In 1960, she was busted in a brothel, and given ninety days in the pokey, but she claimed she was merely visiting a friend there and had no idea it was a house of ill repute. After separating from Axel, she moved to Sacramento, now using the name Sharon Johanson, and in 1968 she married the much younger Roberto Puente. That marriage was a disaster, and it was over by 1969. By now Dorothea was running a boarding house, a white, three-story Victorian gingerbread house on F Street, and acquiring her reputation as a charitable, helpful woman, active in the Spanish-speaking community, whose tidy mansion was a refuge for the poor, the mentally ill, the old people who fell through the cracks of the welfare system.

At forty-seven Dorothea married one last time—*she was never widowed!*—to Pedro Angel Montalvo. This time she gave her father's name as Jesus Sahagun, and her mother's maiden name as Puente. She may have even begun to believe the Mexican heritage she claimed. Her marriage with Pedro lasted a whole week and was eventually annulled.

By 1978, Dorothea was busted again. She'd been stealing her tenants' welfare and Social Security mail, forging their names, and cashing the checks. A kind-hearted judge gave her five years probation and ordered her to pay back the $4,000 she'd stolen. Pedro Montalvo, no longer her husband but still her pal, even helped her make restitution by giving her some of his own money.

Another bust in 1982, and this one was more serious. Dorothea liked to hang out in bars, sipping tall glasses of vodka and grapefruit juice. Sitting at the bar, dressed to kill and sporting good jewelry, she attracted lonely older men the way garbage attracts flies. One day she met a seventy-four-year-old pensioner named Malcolm Mackenzie at a joint called the Zebra Club, slipped a mickey into his drink, went back with him to his apartment, and while he lay helplessly drugged, she helped herself to his valuables, including his ring, which she coolly pulled off his finger. A few months later she drugged and robbed two women, eighty-two and eighty-four years old. Dorothea was arrested, and a plane ticket to Mexico was found in her purse. This time she got four years and was paroled in 1985.

One condition of Dorothea's parole was that she not run any more boarding houses, but that didn't stop her. Once out of prison, Dorothea picked herself up, dusted herself off, and started all over again, this time with a smaller, two-story boarding house further down on F Street. Once again, her boarders were the elderly, alcoholic, and disabled. Nobody bothered looking into Dorothea's past. And anyway, how could this sweet old granny have possibly done anything wrong?

One of the welfare clients sent to Dorothea was a harmless madman named Bert Montoya. This Costa Rican native heard voices, and answered them, loudly. Unable to take care of himself, for years he'd been wandering the streets by day and spending his nights on a mat on the floor of the Sacramento Volunteers of America detox center. By all accounts, Bert, though pretty grungy, was a likable cuss, and even though he wasn't an alcoholic, the VOA staff let him sleep there because he had nowhere else to go, and because they cared about him. VOA street counselor Judy Moise looked for a place to put Bert and found Dorothea. The sweet white-haired boarding house landlady kept a cozy, spotless house, and she really was a great cook. She even had a beautiful garden, which she tended in the extreme early morning hours, before sunrise. Judy Moise gladly placed Bert there.

↜ Dorothea Puente

At first, Dorothea worked wonders on Bert. She cleaned him up, cooked his favorite Mexican food, even got him speaking lucidly sometimes. All in all, life was good for the pathetic tenants of the house on F Street. Many of them had never had a room to themselves, and now they even had television sets in their rooms. Grandmotherly Dorothea made sure they took their medication, and the food was delicious. If one or another of them suddenly disappeared, nobody cared much. After all, these were transients, prone to picking up and moving on.

Then in October 1988, Bert disappeared. Gone to Mexico for a month, Dorothea told his social worker, not to worry, he was staying with her family there. But Bert didn't return. Stayed longer for the fiesta, said Dorothea; then, gone off to live with his brother-in-law in Utah. Brother-in-law? Judy Moise, the social worker, didn't know Bert had a brother-in-law. It was time to call the cops.

Officer Richard Ewing went to the house on F Street and quizzed Dorothea and her tenants. They corroborated her story: that's right, Bert came back from Mexico, but then he left again with his brother-in-law. But one tenant slipped the cop a note that read, "She wants me to lie to you." In private, the tenant related gruesome tales of holes being dug in the garden during pre-dawn hours, and of the stomach-turning stink of rot coming from one room.

On the morning of November 11, 1988, cops rang Dorothea's doorbell. After questioning her they asked, and were given, permission to dig in her garden. Dorothea watched from her doorway as they dug several small holes and found nothing. After an hour of fruitless searching, they were ready to give up when Detective Terry Brown struck pay dirt, about eight inches down.

Actually, what his shovel struck was a human leg bone, encased in a dirty sneaker.

"Oh my lord!" exclaimed Dorothea, watching. She was shocked—shocked!

But the skeleton had been in the ground too long for it to be Bert Montoya, and anyway, it was a woman. There was nothing to pin on Dorothea yet, and the next day the digging continued. By now, word of the grisly find had gotten out, and the house was surrounded by reporters, video cameras, and neighbors in a state of horrified fascination. At around 8:30 A,M. Dorothea, dressed in a pink dress, red coat, and purple pumps, and carrying a matching pink umbrella (it was drizzling) and purple handbag, approached Detective John Cabrera. Would it be all right if she walked down to the Clarion Hotel to have a cup of coffee with her nephew, who worked there? I'm not under arrest, am I? she wanted to know, her voice quavering. There there, little lady, Cabrera reassured her, and he walked her past the bothersome rubberneckers and the TV crews.

Moments after Dorothea disappeared down the street, the second body was found, two feet underground.

The cops actually went to look for Dorothea at the Clarion Hotel! Of course, she was long gone. She had taken a cab to the nearby city of Stockton and bought a plane ticket for Los Angeles, paid for with some of the $3,200 in cash she had stuffed into that matching purple handbag. In Los Angeles, she checked into the Royal Viking Motel, using the name Dorothy Johanson.

She stayed in her room for three days, laying low and venturing out only for takeout food. Meanwhile, five more bodies were dug up in her yard, bringing the total to seven. And the third body was Bert Montoya.

Finally, feeling stir-crazy, or maybe just ready to bounce back as she always had, Dorothea put on her makeup and perfume, fluffed up her white coiffeur, and taxied to a seedy little bar called the Monte Carlo. There, up to her old tricks, she sipped her vodka and grapefruit juice and struck up a conversation with a sixty-seven-year-old pensioner named Charles Willigues. Willigues must have thought he'd died and gone to heaven. Well-bred, well-dressed widows (she said) like Donna Johanson (she said) just didn't frequent places like the Monte Carlo, and certainly had never expressed an interest in him. And this nice fifty-five-year-old lady (she said) had already offered to cook him a nice turkey dinner when Thanksgiving rolled around next week, and was even talking about maybe moving in with him! He started getting a little nervous when she quizzed him on the amount of his pension, but nevertheless made a date with her for the following day.

It wasn't until Willigues got home and turned on the TV news that he got alarmed. He phoned Gene Silver, editor for the

Channel 2 news. Maybe that nice Donna Johanson was the Sacramento landlady the police were looking for? Silver called the cops. Could the police possibly wait until tomorrow night to arrest her, Willigues asked hopefully, after his date with her? No such luck. By 11 P.M., Dorothea was in handcuffs and Willigues was dateless in Los Angeles.

By the time Dorothea's trial actually started in 1993, two more bodies had been added to the count, and she was accused of nine counts of murder. It was the longest trial in the history of California, with 153 people testifying, and the evidence mounting up to 3,500 pages. Yet all the evidence was circumstantial: the bodies had been too decomposed to determine the exact cause of death, although the sedative Dalmane had been found in all of them. But Dalmane is a common prescriptive drug, taken by many people to help them sleep. However, in the right combination with other drugs or alcohol, it can be lethal. This is what the prosecution argued, along with the possibility that Dorothea had drugged her tenants and then simply smothered them with a pillow. Dorothea's defense insisted that all those people had simply died of natural causes, and Dorothy had buried them in her back yard so that she could continue to collect their checks. Sure she's a thief, they said, but she didn't kill anyone.

It took days for a jury to find Dorothea guilty of only three of the nine murders. The jury deadlocked again over whether to give her the death penalty, and when they couldn't reach a decision, the judge sentenced her to life in prison by default.

Dorothea still resides (no, she never had cancer) in the Central California Women's Facility in Chowchilla, California, where she whiles away the hours crafting knick-knacks. She has also written a cookbook in her spare time. She really *was* a good cook!

⨯⨯ ⨯⨯ ⨯⨯ The House on F Street ⨯⨯ ⨯⨯ ⨯⨯

In 2002, Dorothea Puente's house was sold, a bargain at $199,000. The house, built in 1889, is a Victorian beauty, and the neighborhood, once seedy back in the days when Dorothea was planting her tenants in the yard, has become gentrified and very desirable. Naturally, there are rumors that the house is haunted, as would be any house with that many murders connected to it. However, neighbor Alicia Wenbourne told reporters, "Since this neighborhood was built a century ago, there are quite a few people who died in these houses. They just didn't die quite so notoriously."

At the time of this writing, the new owners are renovating the house. One hopes they won't chase away the ghosts.

⨯⨯ The little house of horrors, undergoing renovation *(M. Parfitt, photographer)*

Three

Bandit Queens
and Gun Molls

The Petticoat Terror of the Plains

By the time Myra Maebelle Shirley had become known as Belle Starr, she was already a living legend, written about in scandal sheets of the 1880s like the *Police Gazette,* and the subject of endless speculation. Among her many lovers, it was said, were the infamous bandit Jesse James himself, perhaps his brother Frank, and William Clarke Quantrill, leader of the Civil War guerillas known as Quantrill's Raiders. In fact, these may have been among the only famous outlaws that Belle did *not* sleep with during her violent, action-packed life. She *was* good friends with Jesse, though, and had done a little spying for Quantrill back when she was a teenager and her brother had run away to join the Raiders.

You'd never have known that little Myra, born in 1848 of prosperous, respectable parents—her father, John, owned a city block of business real estate and her mother entertained friends and neighbors by playing and singing genteel songs on the piano—

would end her days shot down by a bushwhacker on a lonely country road. Myra was a good student at the Carthage Female Academy
in Carthage, Missouri, where she learned Greek, Latin, and
Hebrew. Maybe it was the advent of the Civil War, when her father
took sides with the South and her brother ran off with Quantrill,
that Myra discovered the thrill of living outside the law.

Brother Bud got shot down, the South lost the war, and Myra's
daddy lost his business. The family went west, settled in Dallas, and
bought a farm. Men like the James brothers and the Younger
brothers, who'd fought with Quantrill's Raiders alongside brother
Bud, had become outlaws by then, and, perhaps because he felt
it was his patriotic duty as a rebel, daddy John Shirley had a habit
of taking them in when they needed a hideout. Belle—let's call
her Belle now—grown into a pretty eighteen-year-old, met and
fell for Cole Younger, and gave birth to his daughter, Pearl
Younger, in 1866. By that time, Cole had ridden off into the
sunset, although Belle never forgot her first love, and she married another outlaw, Jim Reed.

Well, not exactly *legally* married. Giving refuge to outlaws was
one thing, but Belle's parents didn't want their daughter *marrying* one, so Jim and Belle rode off with his gang, and one of the
gang members performed a wedding ceremony on horseback.
Belle, Jim, and baby Pearl moved in with his folks back in Missouri,
but pretty soon things got too hot for the newlyweds. Jim was

wanted by the law for murder and for selling whiskey to Indians, so the family headed for California, where Belle gave birth to their son, James Edwin. But that goldurned law was still on Jim's trail, and off the family went again, this time back to Texas and a little farm near Scyene. Jim, who apparently just couldn't resist committing crimes, was soon wanted for cattle rustling and two more murders.

This time Belle left the kids with her folks and headed with her man to Indian territory, where Belle may have participated in her first crime, if you don't count poor choice in men. Disguised as a man, but obviously not fooling anybody, Belle, along with Jim and several other outlaws, kidnapped a prospector and hung him from a tree until he told them where he had hidden about $30,000 worth of gold.

By 1874, Jim had a price on his head of $1,500. An ex-gang member of Jim's, John T. Morris, got himself deputized just for the occasion, and shot Jim for the reward. Belle's revenge was to prevent Morris from claiming the money. When asked to identify the corpse, she flatly denied that it was her husband.

Belle, on her own now, became the famed "Bandit Queen," leader of a gang of horse thieves and cattle rustlers operating out of Indian territory in Oklahoma. Among the many lovers or common-law husbands Belle brought to her bed during that period were Bruce Younger, cousin of her first love, Cole, and a whole string of galoots with monikers like Bluford "Blue" Duck, Jim French, and Jack Spaniard.

In 1880, she reportedly forced Bruce Younger to marry her at gunpoint. The happy couple lasted three weeks, after which he took off for points unknown, and she married Sam Starr, a handsome long-haired Indian, and gained the name that was to make her famous. Sam was twenty-three, she was about thirty-two. Belle reclaimed her kids, who'd been living with their grandparents all this time, and the new family settled down in a ranch on Arkansas Indian territory, fifty miles west of Fort Smith. She named her new home Younger's Bend, after the love of her life, Cole Younger, and had a piano shipped in. The couple lived happily, visited from time to time by old friends like Jesse James.

At this point Belle was "discovered" by the Eastern press. The dudes and tenderfeet back East were hungry for tales of the Wild West, and a glamorous bandit queen was just their meat. Penny dreadfuls—cheap pulp adventure books that actually cost a whole dime—about Belle were being published by the dozens, and one-act plays about her were performed all over the country. Belle, who had a flair for the dramatic, actually played herself in one performance at the Sebastian County Fair in Fort Smith, Arkansas. So much was being written about "the petticoat terror of the plains" that it's impossible to separate fact from fiction. One story had her in prison after a bank robbery, and charming the jailer into letting her go. In another tale, enraged after Blue Duck lost $2,000 in what Belle decided was a crooked poker game, she drew a gun on the players and made off with $7,000.

This much is true: Belle dressed in black velvet, rode side-saddle, and was a crack shot with her .45-caliber revolver, which Cole Younger had given to her and which she wore strapped to her hip in an elaborate holster. She was also a lousy mother. She punished her son by horsewhipping him, and broke up a planned marriage between daughter Pearl and the boy she loved, deciding that the boy wasn't good enough for her. Maybe she just didn't want them to turn out like their no-good mom.

If Belle and Sam were living happily, they also, of course, were living a life of crime. They were arrested at least three times: for horse theft, selling whiskey to Indians, and robbing several farms, a case in which Belle, up to her old tricks, disguised herself as a man but was identified by several eye witnesses. Belle was even convicted once and sent to prison for nine months by "hanging judge" Isaac C. Parker.

Sam was usually in even more trouble than Belle, and while he was on the lam from the law, Belle took another lover, John Middleton, nine years younger than she and wanted for arson and murder. Most of her various lovers and husbands seem to have committed at least one murder, so it's a wonder that, in all the literature about Belle, she isn't called a killer. It seems impossible that Belle could have lived her gun-totin', hard-shootin' life without killing anybody, even by accident, and my conclusion is that her nineteenth-century biographers chivalrously declined to sully their heroine's reputation with accusations of murder.

John Middleton didn't last long. His body was found washed up on the banks of the Poteau River, and although the killer was never found, historians don't rule out a jealous Sam Starr. Sam himself didn't last much longer. In 1886, he and a deputy sheriff named Frank West killed each other in a shootout. Belle didn't stay in mourning for long, and by 1887, she had hooked up with another cute Indian, Bill July, at twenty-four almost half her age. They lasted two years, but Belle's time was drawing to a close.

↜ A portrait of the Bandit Queen

In 1889, Bill was wanted on a horse-theft charge (surprise!). Belle convinced him that there was no real evidence against him, and if he surrendered to the authorities at Fort Smith, the case would be thrown out of court. The couple set out for Fort Smith together. Halfway there they separated, Bill going the rest of the way alone, Belle visiting some friends along the way. Belle dined with her friends and departed for home, still nibbling on a piece of cornbread.

She never made it.

The next day, daughter Pearl found Belle's riderless horse in the yard. Alarmed, she rode out to search for her mother and found her lying face down along the road back to Younger's Bend. She had been ambushed and shot in the back, two days before her forty-first birthday. The murderer was never caught, but popular opinion rests on one Edgar Watson, a neighbor who was wanted for murder (surprise, surprise!) in Florida. During an argument with him, Belle had rashly threatened to give him up to the law.

Belle was buried in her favorite black velvet dress, clasping her revolver—Cole Younger's gift—to her breast. The coffin was lined in matching black velvet and trimmed in white lace. Pearl commissioned a gravestone that featured her mother's favorite mare, Venus, and these words:

> *Shed not for her the bitter tear,*
> *Now give the heart to vain regret*
> *Tis but the casket that lies here,*
> *The gem that filled it sparkles yet.*

And Belle's star does indeed still sparkle, in scores of legends, stories, and films, as it has for over a century. About a year before her death, Belle gave an interview to a journalist from the *Fort Smith Elevator,* which included this understatement: "I regard myself as a woman who has seen much of life."

↤↤↤↤ The Movie ↦↦↦↦

Actually, you'd expect to find more movies about America's infamous lady bandit. Although Belle played a peripheral role in many a Western, I could only track down three movies featuring her name in the title, and one of them, *Belle Starr's Daughter,* is about Pearl avenging her mom's death. Unlike the film's heroine, played by Ruth Roman, the real Pearl didn't do so well, becoming first a prostitute and then a madame.

Elizabeth Montgomery played Belle in a 1980s movie made for TV, but good luck finding that. Easier to track down in your more complete video stores is Lina Wertmuller's 1967 spaghetti Western, *The Belle Starr Story.* Don't look for authenticity in this one, but Italian bombshell Elsa Martinelli, as a bandit queen with mod raccoon eye makeup and black leather pants is a hoot. In one scene, she even wears hip-hugging pantaloons.

Best of the lot is Gene Tierney's 1941 flick simply called *Belle Starr*. In her wildest dreams, Belle never looked this good, and the scriptwriters have mixed Sam Starr up with Quantrill, but who cares? The film is shot in early Technicolor, and if you can find it on late-night TV, I give it two thumbs up.

REWARD

$10,000

IN GOLD COIN

Will be paid by the U. S. Government for the apprehension

DEAD OR ALIVE

of

SAM and BELLE STARR

Wanted for Robbery, Murder, Treason and other acts against the peace and dignity of the U. S.

THOMAS CRAIL

Major, 8th Missouri Cavalry, Commanding

"Tell Them I Don't Smoke Cigars"

What can you say about a girl who wasn't even five feet tall, weighed 90 pounds, wrote poetry, and died young, riddled with bullets and with a machine gun in her lap?

Bonnie Parker grew up in the depressingly named Cement City, Texas. She was a cute'n'perky little thang, acting in school plays and singing with the choir at First Baptist Church, and she loved to write. She was a romantic. In another location, at another time, she might have become a writer of romances, another Danielle Steele, but the poor kid was doomed by the place and the age she lived in. Like true Texas white trash, Bonnie quit school at sixteen to marry a handsome no-account named Roy Thornton, who had a roving eye and, anyway, wound up in the slammer. To no one's surprise, despite the fact that Bonnie had Roy's name tattooed above her right knee, the marriage didn't last. The couple never did get officially divorced, but by the time

Bonnie was riding with the infamous Barrow Gang, legal marriage was the least of her problems.

Bonnie was a researcher's dream come true. She kept a diary! In December 1927, she wrote:

> Before opening this year's diary, I wish to tell you that I have a roaming husband with a roaming mind. We are separated again for the third and last time. . . . I am running around with Rosa Mary Judy and she is somewhat of a consolation to me. We have resolved this New Year's to take no men or nothing seriously. Let all men go to hell!

Bonnie tried to forget her sorrows in movies—she went almost every day—but comparing her bleak existence in hardscrabble Cement City to the glamour on the silver screen made her even more miserable. Some of her diary entries:

> *January 1, 1928*
>
> I went to a show. Saw Ken Maynard in *The Overland Stage.* Am very blue. Well, I must confess this New Year's nite I got drunk. . . . Drowning my sorrows in bottled hell!

> *Jan. 2, 1928*
>
> Met Rosa Mary today and we went to a show. Saw Ronald Coleman and Vilma Banky in *A Night of Love.* Sure was a good show. . . . Sure am lonesome.

Jan. 12, 1928

Went to a show. Saw Florence Vidor and Clive Brook in *Afraid
to Love.* Sure was good. Blue as hell tonight.

Jan. 13, 1928

Went to a show. Saw Virginia Vallie in *Marriage.* Not a thing
helps out though. Sure am blue. . . . Why don't something
happen? What a life!

"Something" happened in 1929. It was the first year of the
Great Depression, and seventeen-year-old Bonnie was a waitress.
She'd been working at Marco's Cafe in downtown Dallas, where
she often "forgot" to charge the gaunt-faced unemployed men
who tried to forget their troubles for a half-hour, hunched over
a cup of hot java and a slice of pie. Marco's probably would have
gone bankrupt anyway, and when it closed, she moved on to the
American Cafe, a block from the Dallas County courthouse.
The cute little strawberry blonde was a hit with the customers, and
among the men who showed up at the American Cafe, possibly
hoping for more than a cuppa joe from the pert waitress, was a
young cop named Ted Hinton. In later life he would recall that
she'd confided to him that "she wanted to be a singer . . . or
maybe an actress or poet."

But the fates had another future planned for Bonnie, and, although the two would meet again some day, that future didn't include Ted Hinton. Bonnie met the man she'd spend the rest of her life with at a girlfriend's house just before Christmas 1929. His name was Clyde Chestnut Barrow, and he was wanted by the law.

Clyde was one of eight kids from a family that was often homeless when he was younger. While he was still a teenager, Clyde and his big brother Buck earned the nickname "The Terrible Barrows" by hanging out in pool halls and committing various minor crimes. One night they stole an entire safe from the Motor Mark Garage, loaded it into their flivver, and promptly crashed the car into a lamppost. Clyde escaped the pursuing cops, but Buck was caught, arrested for burglary, and sent to prison. The night after his brother's arrest, Clyde was back at it, burglarizing a store in Waco, along with some pals.

Clyde had slicked-back brown hair, and the ladies liked him. He liked to brag to them about the lawless exploits he'd gotten away with, but it was only a matter of time before the authorities decided to investigate Clyde and his gang of toughs. He was arrested on February 12, 1930, and sent to the Waco County courthouse to await trial. Bonnie inundated her sweetie with letters:

February 14, 1930

Sugar, when you do get out, I want you to go to work, and for God's sake, don't get into any more trouble. . . . Sugar, when you get clear and don't have to run, we can have some fun. . . .

Honey, I sure wish I was with you tonight. I'm so lonesome for you, dearest. . . . Sugar, I never knew I really cared for you until you got into jail. And honey, if you get out o.k., please don't ever do anything to get locked up again. If you ever do, I'll get me a railroad ticket fifty miles long and let them tear off an inch every thousand miles, because I never did want to love you. . . .

Bonnie visited Clyde in prison and smuggled in a gun. Her brown-haired "sugar" and his cellmate, Frank Turner, escaped that night. Texas now being too hot for them, they headed for Illinois in a series of stolen cars, committing petty crimes for small cash along the way. It was only a matter of time before Clyde was caught again and sent back to the Waco County slammer for a speedy trial. Sentenced to an infamous Texas prison farm, rife with ghastly working conditions, beatings, and homosexuality, Clyde got out of that one by arranging an "accident" in which he lost two toes. He was out on parole and limping into Bonnie's arms by February 1932. And this time, Bonnie was with him for good.

Well, not quite for good. A month after Clyde was released, after one of their first attempted burglaries, Bonnie was arrested. Awaiting trial in a Kaufman, Texas, prison cell, feeling deserted by Clyde, who didn't dare contact her for fear of the law, she composed and wrote down the first of her two now-famous poems, "The Story of Suicide Sal." Bonnie's poems are folk poetry, written by someone who was obviously familiar with bluegrass ballads and popular pulp fiction, and she has an excellent sense of rhythm and rhyme. Three months later, Bonnie was acquitted for lack of evidence, and this time, for the reunited lovers, it was "till death do we part."

While Bonnie had been rotting in her jail cell, Clyde, in a botched robbery, accidentally killed his first man. It was too late now for Bonnie's admonishments not to get into any more trouble. She and her man started down a road that could have only one end. Teaming up with various henchmen at various times, the Barrow Gang, as they were dubbed by the newspapers of the day, cut a swath through the South, the West, and the Midwest, robbing whatever was robbable, from trains, gas stations, and groceries to banks, making spectacular getaways in fast stolen cars, and killing too many cops during their shootouts with the law. Bonnie was as guilty as the others. She was a crack shot and proud of it, and when the bullets were flying, nobody really could say who was responsible for hitting whom. Bonnie justified all of this: it was their lives or hers and her "sugar."

In March 1933, Buck got out of jail and joined the gang, dragging along his pretty but unwilling red-haired wife, Blanche, and her little white doggie, too. Blanche was more of a liability than a help. The two couples rented a furnished apartment, attempting a vacation from crime, but in April, cops, tipped off by neighbors who'd seen the Barrow boys unloading their arsenal, converged on the place. The Barrow Gang and the law exchanged fire, and two cops fell dead. Blanche, in a fit of hysteria, screamed and fled. The gang made it to their garage and piled into their car, with Clyde, as usual, at the wheel. He floored the gas pedal and the car burst through the garage straight into the gaggle of cops, who leaped out of the way to avoid being run over. Stopping only long enough to snatch Blanche, who stood across the street, still screaming, her little white dog tucked into her pocket, Clyde performed another of his miraculous escapes.

Back in the apartment, the cops found rolls of film that yielded the famous photo of Bonnie in a stylish sweater set, squinting into the sun, her strawberry blonde hair tucked into a beret, her dainty feet in MaryJanes, leaning on the bumper of a car, a gun in her hand and a cigar in her mouth. She was only playing tough— she and Clyde loved to clown for their Kodak Brownie box camera—but the newspapers had a field day, pinning every unsolved crime on the pair. They called Bonnie a "hard, straight-shooting,

↬ Bonnie and the famous cigar

boasting female gangster" and Clyde's "cigar-smoking, quick-shooting woman accomplice." Bonnie hated it, and once, after they kidnapped an Oklahoma police chief, took him on a wild ride, and then released him in Kansas, she asked him to pass the word to the press: "Tell them I don't smoke cigars."

Bonnie had become a romantic figure; she should have loved it. The dirt-poor Depression years spawned many an outlaw, from Pretty Boy Floyd and Baby Face Nelson to John Dillinger. All were glorified and romanticized by the American public, but none had a girlfriend who was a gun-toting outlaw in her own right like Bonnie.

The truth is, Bonnie and Clyde were losers, though you'd never know it from the publicity they got. Times were hard, money was scarce, and the Barrow Gang often survived on nickels and dimes gleaned from cash registers in down-and-out mom'n'pop stores. Their bank robberies were singularly unsuccessful. From one bank they made off with the spectacular sum of $80, and they broke into another bank only to find that it was empty, having folded weeks before. They slept in their cars, in open fields, or in a succession of dinky motel rooms. Only Clyde's death-defying, escape-artist driving got them out of their various close calls with the law.

Through it all, Bonnie and Clyde managed to stay nattily dressed, as can be seen in their photos. Clyde favored sharp pinstriped suits and snap-brimmed hats. Bonnie liked to wear red. And through it all, they tried to see their families when they could, though this often meant hurried rendezvous in fields and forests, too soon broken up by the appearance of a patrol car.

After their spectacular escape from the law in April 1933, things started to go wrong for the Barrow Gang. Driving down the highway toward a ravine, they missed a sign warning that a bridge was out. Too late, Clyde jammed on the brakes, but the car spun and turned over into the water below. Bonnie tumbled from the car and was pinned under it, just as a fire started in the engine. Clyde and the gang managed to drag her free just before the car exploded, but she was badly cut and burned. A nearby farm family took them in, but the farmer couldn't help noticing the arsenal that spilled out of the car, and he tipped off the cops. Clyde loaded the semi-conscious Bonnie into the farmer's car and pulled off another Houdini-esque escape. They hid out at a tourist camp and stole a doctor's car, gaining his bag full of painkillers, gauze, and dressings. Miraculously, Bonnie survived and started to heal.

It got worse on the evening of July 18, 1933, when the gang rented two cabins at the Red Crown Tourist Camp near Platte City, Missouri. The night clerk took one look at the three heavily armed men half-carrying the woman with a bandaged leg and phoned the highway patrol. Police Capt. William Baxter remembered that Bonnie Parker had been badly hurt in an auto accident the month before, and gathered together his own county cops and the Platte City police department. The next night, an army of lawmen in armored cars bore down on the tourist camp, and this time they were ready. The cops met Clyde's and Buck's guns with a barrage of bullets that tore the little cabins apart. Two bullets pierced Buck's skull. Blood pouring down his face, he fell into Blanche's arms. Carrying Bonnie, Clyde led the gang into the garage and their car, and once more drove hell-bent for leather, straight through the assembled cops. As the car sped away, a couple of cops shook off their state of shock long enough to shoot through the auto's rear window, right where Blanche sat with Buck in her lap. She screamed as shards of glass pierced her right eye, blinding her.

Clyde pulled into a small forest park, and the gang nursed their wounds, but by morning they'd been spotted by a hunter who alerted the sheriff's office. Soon the fugitives were surrounded by more than a hundred heavily armed men. Their escape car shot out from under them, Bonnie and Clyde fled into the forests and the fields, leaving behind the dying Buck and his blinded wife, who'd never wanted to be an outlaw anyway. He died in the hospital; she got ten years in prison.

The lawless lovers hid out for the next months, emerging long enough to rob a payroll office. But they needed henchmen. In January 1934 they broke a buddy of Clyde's out of jail. His cellmate Henry Methvin, a car thief, came along for the ride, and the Barrow Gang was complete again. More holdups followed, more shootouts, and more cops killed. There was only one way their story could end, and Bonnie knew it.

Bonnie and Clyde arranged one last meeting with their families on a lonely country road, on May 6, 1934. She told her mother, "Mama, when they kill us, don't let them take me to an undertaking parlor, will you? Bring me home. . . . I want to lie in the front room. . . . A long, cool, peaceful night

↬ On this cover from the 1940s comic, *Crimes by Women*, the artist hasn't made an attempt to draw the real Bonnie Parker—even her hair color is wrong!

together before I leave you." And she handed her mother a poem she had written, "The Story of Bonnie and Clyde."

It was coming. The gang headed to Acadia, Louisiana, to hide out at the home of Henry Methvin's father, Iverson. But Methvin was having second thoughts. A small-time hood, he was in over his head. He confessed to his father, and Iverson got in touch with Police Chief Tom Bryan to offer a trade: clemency for his son in return for Bonnie and Clyde. On the morning of May 23, 1934, a posse waited on a country road for Clyde's gray 1934 Ford sedan. Leading them was bounty hunter Frank Hamer, a former Texas ranger who'd been tracking the couple for years. Speeding down the road, Clyde spotted Iverson's beat-up truck, seemingly stalled by the roadside, and slowed down. Hamer gave the command: "Shoot!" The posse pumped 167 bullets into the car, which careened out of control into an embankment. Fifty bullets struck the doomed couple.

One member of the ambush posse was Ted Hinton, Bonnie's young admirer from the days when she waitressed at the American Cafe, and now a Dallas County deputy sheriff. He ran to the bullet-riddled car. Clyde was slumped over the wheel, Hinton remembered, "the back of his head a mat of blood." He pulled open the door on the passenger's side. Bonnie Parker, her stylish red dress soaked with darker blood, fell into his arms.

She was twenty-three years old.

❀❀❀❀ **The Movie** ❀❀❀❀

Almost before their bodies cooled, Hollywood was turning out films inspired by Bonnie Parker and Clyde Barrow. The first, *You Only Live Twice,* was made in 1937. Henry Fonda and Sylvia Sydney, as the doomed lovers, get mowed down by the law in a swamp, surrounded by evocative mist.

Gun Crazy, made fifteen years later, has an oddly similar ending, swamp mists and all, but beautiful Peggy Cummins plays crackshot heroine Annie Laurie Starr as criminally insane, and, unlike the real Bonnie Parker, the instigator of the couple's life of crime.

Finally, in 1967, producer Warren Beatty and director Arthur Penn made *Bonnie and Clyde,* and did it right, almost. Some of the movie is odd; the film hints that Clyde was either impotent or gay, yet there doesn't seem to be any evidence of this in any of the histories I've read. Faye Dunaway, as Bonnie, is about a foot taller than the real thing, and looks like she stepped out of the pages of a 1967 *Vogue* magazine, but she does a great Texas accent.

And the ending, even when you know what's coming, is shocking and heartbreaking.

✦✦✦✦ **The Ballad** ✦✦✦✦

Here's Bonnie's ballad, as written down in a calendar by Clyde Barrow.

THE STORY OF BONNIE AND CLYDE

by Bonnie Parker

You've read the story of Jesse James -
Of how he lived and died;
If you're still in need
Of something to read
Here's the story of Bonnie and Clyde.

Now Bonnie and Clyde are the Barrow gang.
I'm sure you all have read
How they rob and steal
And those who squeal
Are usually found dying or dead.

There's lots of untruths to those writeups;
They're not as ruthless as that;
Their nature is raw;
They hate all the law -
The stool pigeons, spotters, and rats.

They call them cold-blooded killers;
They say they are heartless and mean;
But I say with pride,

That I once knew Clyde
When he was honest and upright and clean.

But the laws fooled around,
Kept taking him down
And locking him up in a cell,
Till he said to me,
"I'll never be free,
So I'll meet a few of them in hell."

The road was so dimly lighted;
There were no highway signs to guide;
But they made up their minds
If all roads were blind,
They wouldn't give up till they died.

The road gets dimmer and dimmer;
Sometimes you can hardly see;
But it's fight, man to man,
And do all you can,
For they know they can never be free.

If a policeman is killed in Dallas,
And they have no clue or guide;
If they can't find a fiend,
They just wipe their slate clean
And hang it on Bonnie and Clyde.

A newsboy once told his buddy:
"I wish old Clyde would get jumped;
In these awful hard times
We'd make a few dimes
If five or six cops would get bumped."

If they try to act like citizens
And rent them a nice little flat,
About the third night
They're invited to fight
By a sub-gun's rat-tat-tat.

They don't think they're too smart or desperate,
They know that the law always wins;
They've been shot at before,
But they do not ignore
That death is the wages of sin.

Some day they'll go down together;
They'll bury them side by side;
To a few it'll be grief -
To the law a relief -
But it's death for Bonnie and Clyde.

Monday, July 17, 1933

198th day—167 days to come

*youve read the story of Jesse James
of how he lived and died
if youre still in need
of something to read
heres the story of Bonnie & Clyde*

The Pirate Queen of Macau

In South China of the 1920s and 1930s, the island of Macau was a den of thieves and cutthroats. Pirates ruled the China seas, and any vessel sailed there at its own risk. Many of these ships hired White Russian guards for protection and barred their engine rooms, but this didn't stop the pirates, who were after silver dollars, which was legal tender in China at the time. If there was no silver to be found, the unfortunate passengers might find themselves kidnapped and held for ransom. If the ransom money was slow in coming, first an ear or a finger, then perhaps an entire hand, might be sent to the victim's relatives to help loosen their purse strings.

Side by side with the pirates sprang up another industry—a seaborne protection racket. These were semilegal pirates, who solicited—and got—protection money from the various junks and fishing fleets. (Of course, ships that didn't come across with money were liable to meet with "accidents.") In return for their payoffs, the "protectors" policed the waters around Macau, meting out a cruel justice upon any pirates they might come in contact with, and often fighting bloody battles with other would-be protectors who trespassed on their watery turf. The undisputed leader of these avenging marauders was a woman: Lai Choi San, the Pirate Queen of Macau.

Lai Choi San's name meant "Mountain of Wealth," and she was indeed filthy rich. Her father, who had also been a pirate, expected eventually to turn his business over to his four sons. Still, he took young Lai along on his excursions to perform "woman's work" for him, mending his clothes and cooking. The girl got used to life on the water, and after her father and her four brothers all died "with their slippers on," meaning in combat, she inherited the family's seven ships. By the late 1920s, she had built her fleet up to twelve and owned a mansion in Macau. She had a reputation as something of a Robin Hood to the fisher folk she protected, but to her enemies she was fierce and ruthless.

At the same time, Lai was very much a woman, and a mother. She'd been married twice—her first husband was killed by a rival gang—and had many lovers. She liked to take her young son along on her excursions. She was training the kid to eventually take over the family business and boasted proudly that he already smoked like a man. Sailing with some of the toughest guys on the

China coast, Lai was careful to preserve her reputation. A pirate queen she might be, but never a loose woman, so she always traveled with two *amahs,* Cantonese chaperones.

Much of what we know about Lai Choi San is from a book called *I Sailed with Chinese Pirates,* written in 1930 by a Finnish adventurer named Aleko Lilius. A real-life Indiana Jones, Lilius paid Lai $43 a day for the privilege of sailing with her on raids in her heavily armored junk. In his book, Lilius supplies a vivid description of the pirate queen:

> What a woman she was! Rather slender and short, her hair jet black, with jade pins gleaming in the knot at the neck, her ear-rings and bracelets of the same precious apple-green stone. She was exquisitely dressed in a white satin robe fastened with green jade buttons and green silk slippers. . . . Her face and dark eyes were intelligent. . . .

But when she dressed for action on her ship, she tossed the glamour garb overboard. Lilius writes that "she was entirely transformed. Now she wore a jacket-like blouse and black trousers made of the strong, glossy material commonly used by coolies for garments. Her two amahs were dressed in a similar fashion." And both Lai and her chaperones carried rifles and strapped cartridge belts around their waists.

On board her ships, Lai was an empress, never deigning to

speak to the crew, but barking her orders only to the captain himself. And she was *always* obeyed!

Lilius was on board Lai's ship when she battled a rival gang, but the captain forced him to hide below in his cabin. All he could do was listen as six shots were fired from Lai's ship, with no answering shots from the foe. He was allowed back up on deck in time to see the rival ship sinking and to find two men lying on the deck, bound hand and foot. They would not be killed, he was told. It was more profitable to ransom them back to their families.

Although Lai was an officially government-sanctioned "protector," she doesn't seem to have been above the occasional act of pure piracy. In 1928, a steamer called the SS *Anking* was attacked by pirates led by a woman. The captain and five officers were shot, and the captain later died of his wounds. Although it was never proved, Lai was probably the woman in charge of the attack.

Brigand she might be, but Lai Choi San was a patriot, too, and the Japanese were her sworn enemies. By the late 1920s, the Japanese had already invaded China and had set up a puppet government in Manchukuo, and Lai set her sights on the Japanese fleet. When the Japanese ship *Delhi Maru* was attacked by pirates on September 20, 1929, and several of the guards were shot, the newspapers reported that the raid had been "led by a woman pirate." Of course, everyone knew that there was only one woman pirate who could have done the deed.

Nobody knows what eventually happened to the Pirate Queen of Macau, although one source suggests she may have been executed by the Japanese in 1939. But that wasn't the end for Chinese women pirates. Lai's successor was Huang Pemei, Madame Two Revolvers, who worked for Chiang Kai-Shek and the American Secret Service during the Second World War.

I prefer to believe that Lai survived the war, retired, and enjoyed her wealth, living to a ripe old age in her Macau mansion along with her aging amahs, dressing in jade and satin, and burning incense in front of her statue of A-Ma, the goddess of the sea.

↬ From a 1940s magazine story about Lai Choi San. The artist probably never saw a photo of the real woman.

❧❧❧❧ The Dragon Lady ❧❧❧❧

When cartoonist Milton Caniff started his long-running comic strip, *Terry and the Pirates,* in 1934, Lai Choi San still ruled the South China coast. Caniff's strip took place in China, and although the cartoonist had never been there, he researched his subject thoroughly. He was influenced by movies as well as by then-current news coming out of China. For instance, his blonde-bombshell character, Burma, was obviously based on Jean Harlow in the movie, *China Seas.* But for his glamorous Chinese pirate queen, the Dragon Lady, whose name has become synonymous with Asian vamps, he chose Lai Choi San. Described in the strip as "the most notorious woman pirate on the China coast," the ruthless Dragon Lady's sworn enemies, like those of her inspiration, were the Japanese invaders. But she had a soft spot in her heart for the adventurer Pat Ryan, who may or may not have been based on Aleko Lilius. At any rate, Lilius's son tried unsuccessfully to sue the strip's publishers.

We don't know if Lai Choi San ever saw the comic strip, but if she did, she probably liked it.

↬ Lai Choi San as the Dragon Lady in *Terry and the Pirates* by Milton Caniff, 1934.

India's Bandit Queen

Of all the killers in this book, only Phoolan Devi seems justified in her acts. The illiterate daughter of a low-caste fisherman in a remote mud-hut village in the Central India province of Uttar Pradesh, at the age of eleven Phoolan was married off to a man three times her age. Her husband paid the price of a cow and a bicycle for his new bride, and beat and raped her. No matter how "legal" a marriage between an eleven-year-old child and a grown man may be, any sex between them can only be considered rape.

After a year of this treatment, the young girl ran away, hiking alone over an area roughly as wide as Texas, to return home. In traditional villages like Phoolan's, it is a disgrace for a woman to leave her husband, and Phoolan was considered to be no better than a prostitute. Her mother even suggested that the only way to save the family's honor would be for her daughter to commit suicide. Phoolan did not kill herself, but matured into an attractive young woman. The upper-caste men of her village harassed her constantly.

India's 2,500-year-old caste system is its own form of apartheid or segregation. You are born into a caste from which there is no escape. Your caste defines how you will live, what you will eat and wear, where you will be allowed to stand at the village well, even whether or not you will be allowed to enter a temple. If lower-caste men are considered inferior by the higher castes, lower-caste women have it even worse: they are sexual targets. In a 1996 interview with journalist Mary Anne Weaver, Phoolan grimly explained, "It is assumed that the daughters of the poor are for the use of the rich. They assume that we're their property. . . . We can't cut the grass or tend to the crops without being accosted by them. We are the property of the rich."

In 1979, Phoolan, now twenty-one years old, complained to the village authorities, but it was she who was put into prison for a month, where as a matter of course she was beaten and raped by her guards. Soon after her release from prison, a gang of bandits, known in India as *dacoits,* invaded her parents' home and dragged her off with them. An upper-caste relative of the Devis, whom Phoolan had accused of stealing land from her father, may have paid the gang to get rid of his trouble-making cousin. Or perhaps the upper-caste dacoit leader, Babu Gujar, had decided to punish this uppity, tradition-breaking woman whom he considered a low-caste whore. In any case, Phoolan was force-marched into the ravines where the bandits made their lairs, and was raped by the bandit chief for the next three days. Finally,

Gujar's chief lieutenant, Vikram Mallah, a handsome young l ow-caste man who took pity on Phoolan, shot his chief and took over leadership of the gang. He and Phoolan became lovers: he taught her to negotiate the steep hills and valleys of the Indian badlands, and he taught her to shoot. He also told her: "If you are going to kill, kill twenty, not just one. For if you kill twenty, your fame will spread; if you kill only one, they will hang you as a murderess."

For the next year, the lovers and their gang roamed the hills and snake-infested jungles of Uttar and Madhya Pradesh, looting, robbing trains, stealing from upper-caste villagers, and killing a goodly number of them along the way. But always before they attacked and ransacked another village, Phoolan would visit a temple to Durga, where she would kneel before her patron goddess, whom she believed protected her and gave her strength. Her battle cry was *"Jai Durga Mata!"* ("Victory to Durga, the Mother Goddess!").

As Phoolan's fame spread among lower-caste villagers, especially among the women, she was soon considered a reincarnation of Durga herself. Songs were written about her, and legends grew up around her. One such tale had her climbing to the roof of a bank her gang was robbing, singing to the people on the street below, and bewitching them all, including the police. Vikram Mallah was in for his share of fame, too, as a lower-caste man who had dared to kill his upper-caste chief and take over the gang. Phoolan was called the Beautiful Bandit, the Rebel of the Ravines, the Goddess of Flowers, but she had her own name for herself. She commissioned a rubber stamp. She couldn't read it, but she knew what it said: "Phoolan Devi, dacoit beauty, beloved of Vikram Mallah, Emperor of Dacoits."

Late one August night in 1980, Phoolan and Vikram were camped in the jungle when a shot rang out. Vikram had been shot; he died with his head in his lover's lap. His killers were Sri Ram and Lala Ram, upper-caste dacoit brothers who had just been released from prison, and who were avenging the death of Babu Gujar. Phoolan was overpowered and bound, tossed like a sack of flour into the bottom of a boat, which sailed down the Yamuna River to the village of Behmai, home

↜ The Hindu Goddess Durga. Many people believed that Phoolan was a reincarnation of Durga

to about fifty families of Thakurs, one of India's highest castes. As much as the lower castes idolized her, Phoolan was hated and feared by the upper castes, especially the men.

In Behmai, Phoolan was held captive in a dark, filthy hut for three weeks. Every night, turbaned upper-caste men whose faces she could not see took turns raping her until she fainted. Finally, she was dragged outside by the dacoit brothers, who forced her to parade nude in front of the laughing, jeering Thakur men of Behmai.

Rescued by a priest from a nearby village, Phoolan recovered and formed her own gang. This young woman, not even five feet tall, became the Avenging Angel of the Ravines, leading her gang of upper-caste dacoits. Most untraditionally, she cropped her hair, wore lipstick and nail polish, and dressed in jeans and boots. She earned the reputation of a female Robin Hood who looted the rich to help the poor. You could even buy a Phoolan Devi doll.

And of course the upper-caste men continued to hate her, and as before, they attacked her sexuality, accusing her of being a nymphomaniac. One police inspector said, "For every man this girl has killed, she has slept with two. Sometimes she sleeps with them first, before she bumps them off." A rival upper-caste dacoit called her a woman of loose character. Naturally, none of these men made mention of how many women they had slept with—or raped—or how many more women they would sleep with if given half the chance.

A deputy police commandant explained to journalist Mary Ann Weaver why people become dacoits: "Some join for reasons of revenge: if the system gives you no justice, then you take justice into your own hands." Phoolan definitely took justice into her own hands, and she had her revenge.

On Saint Valentine's Day 1981, Phoolan and her gang invaded Behmai, dragging about thirty Thakur men from their homes, lining them up and demanding that they reveal Sri Ram's and Lala Ram's hideout. When they denied all knowledge of the dacoit brothers, Phoolan strode up and down the line, ripping off their turbans in a fury, beating them with the butt of her rifle while they begged for mercy. Finally, the men were marched down to the river where they were forced to kneel. Shots rang out and twenty-two of the men fell dead. This largest massacre in modern India, led by a lower-caste woman, was dubbed "The Saint Valentine's Day Massacre." Phoolan wasn't yet twenty-six years old.

She had avenged her rape by the men of Behmai, but there was one small problem: Phoolan had no way of knowing if these really had been the men who raped her, or merely those who jeered and spat as she was paraded naked in front of them. It didn't matter to her; she felt vindicated. But now things got hot for her. She had gone too far, and important upper-caste men insisted on her capture. There was a price of $10,400 on her head.

Phoolan managed to elude the law for two more years before surrendering in February 1983. With a red scarf tied around her flowing dark hair and a small silver figurine of the goddess Durga tucked into her breast pocket, she mounted the wooden steps of a twenty-three-foot-high dais and knelt before the portraits of Gandhi and Durga that she had insisted on as a condition of her surrender. A watching crowd of 8,000 people cheered her. Even in surrender, she was a legend.

Eleven years later, after having been held in prison without benefit of a trial, Phoolan was finally pardoned by Uttar Pradesh's new chief minister, himself a member of the lower castes. That same year, a film about Phoolan, *The Bandit Queen,* was released to excellent reviews, and was quickly banned in India, where censors objected to the movie's graphic sex and its depiction of India's caste system.

In 1996, Phoolan authored an autobiography and was elected to Parliament in India by a landslide. Campaigning against the caste system and promising to work for the "upliftment of women, the downtrodden, and the poor," she earned yet another name: The Gandhi of Mirzapur. Now a respected member of Parliament, Phoolan settled down in a modest three-story house in New Delhi, with a husband, Umed Singh, a high-caste realtor whom it was rumored she called "my wife." New York performance artist Penny Arcade interviewed Phoolan, asking why she had married. She answered that she was worried about what people would think of her, and that she needed protection. Penny couldn't believe what she heard. She exploded, "Phoolan, you killed twenty-two men, and you're worried about what people will think of you?"

But Phoolan did need protection. After she was elected to Parliament, the government reduced her bodyguards from ten policemen to only one, even though she constantly received death threats. On July 25, 2001, she was ambushed by three masked gunmen as she returned home from a morning session of Parliament. They wounded her sole bodyguard and pumped five bullets into her. She was rushed to a hospital and pronounced dead.

Phoolan's assassins were Thakurs, bent on revenge for the Saint Valentine's Day Massacre. But Phoolan lives on in songs and stories among exploited Indian women. Illiterate, raped, and abused, she avenged herself and rose from legal slavery at the age of eleven to a place in India's Parliament. Yet at the time of her surrender, Phoolan had told reporters, "What do I know about, except using a rifle and cutting grass?"

↝↝↝↝ The Movie ↝↝↝↝

Phoolan's life story, *The Bandit Queen,* was released to rave reviews in 1994 and immediately ran into trouble. The Indian government banned it, and Phoolan didn't like it much, either. Although the film is excellently acted, beautifully photographed, and packs a wallop, Phoolan objected to the unsettling rape scenes and the shots of actress Seema Biswas, as Phoolan, being paraded nude in front of the villagers. When the board of censors rescinded their ban, Phoolan sued and threatened to set herself on fire in front of the theater if the film was shown. Eventually she was mollified by the offer of an out-of-court settlement of £40,000.

In an online chat at indya.com, the Bandit Queen explained her feelings: "I did not want the naked scenes to be depicted on screen. A lot of women from impoverished backgrounds undergo this humiliation. Several such women even commit suicide. Only some of us have the strength to fight back."

↜ Phoolan Devi and New York performance artist Penny Arcade in 1995

Four

Fabled
Femmes Fatales

The Woman Who Isn't in the Painting

The original painting by Jacques-Louis David hangs in the Royal Museum in Brussels, but you've probably seen it in an art book. A turban wound around his head, the man in the painting slumps lifelessly in his cloth-draped bathtub. His right arm, hanging outside the tub, still holds a quill pen; a list rests in his left hand. The painting is called *The Death of Marat,* but the most important person in the story it tells is not in the picture. A portrait of that person, done while she awaited execution in prison, shows a pretty girl with typically French heavy eyelids and long, straight nose. A fashionable mob cap perches on her long dark curls. Her name was Charlotte Corday. She was Marat's assassin, and she was twenty-four years old.

Marie Anne Charlotte Corday D'Armont was born in 1768. Her family were aristocrats, but not the kind who had bankrupted France, starved her citizens, and who, after the revolution, were losing their heads to La Guillotine while the mob cheered. In fact, they were poor, though in decent enough financial condition to have their daughter brought up properly in a convent in Caen, Normandy.

She was well read, well bred, and romantic. Among her ancestors was the famous dramatist Pierre Corneille, who is considered the father of French tragedy. The lessons in his plays were basically that, no matter what the personal cost, a man's gotta do what a man's (or woman's) gotta do. Charlotte devoured the works of philosopher Jean-Jacques Rousseau, a major influence on both the French Revolution and the then-current romantic movement. His recurring theme was that politics and morality must never be separated. All in all, Charlotte was an enlightened woman by the standards of her day. Aristocrat or not, she approved of the revolution and supported the Girondists, political moderates who could be compared to the American Democratic Party.

On the other hand, Marat's political affiliation, the Jacobin Party, can be compared to the most hard-core Maoists during the Chinese Cultural Revolution of the 1960s. The Jacobins, the original terrorists, were responsible for the mass atrocities and beheadings that we now call the Reign of Terror, which followed the French Revolution. Ironically, the Jacobins, too, invoked the name of Rousseau to justify their Stalinist-type purges. Marat was a journalist who wielded such power through his newspaper,

The Friend of the People, that even revolutionary leaders like Danton and Robespierre feared him. Among the many victims of his denunciations were King Louis XVI and the entire Girondist Party.

As early as 1789, when Marat had twenty-two Girondists arrested, Charlotte considered killing him. She wrote, over and over again, on little slips of paper, "Shall I or shall I not?" It took her a while to completely make up her mind. The king's execution in January 1793 was the last straw for Charlotte, who wasn't so liberal that she didn't support the monarchy.

By this time, the expelled Girondists had taken refuge in Caen, and Charlotte was hanging out with them. The horror stories they told about Marat, Paris, and the Terror must have helped her make her final decision. She packed up her dreams and went to Paris, leaving behind her Bible open to the story of Judith, the Jewish heroine who saved her people by beheading the Assyrian general Holofernes. No doubt she also thought about that other romantic young French girl, Joan of Arc. Like Joan, she too would become the savior of her country.

Charlotte arrived in Paris and bought a kitchen knife. She had considered emulating the Roman hero Brutus and stabbing Marat through the heart on the floor of the French Senate, the way Brutus had dispatched Julius Caesar. However, Marat wasn't attending the Senate for the time being. He suffered from a nasty skin condition that forced him to spend most of his time in bathwater full of healing herbs. The tub, draped with a sheet for modesty's sake, was where he conducted most of his business.

She sent him a note saying she had news of a planned Girondist uprising in Caen. Girondist uprisings were Marat's meat. He agreed to see her on July 13, 1793. Seated in his bathtub, he copied down the names of the Girondists as she dictated them to him. Suddenly Charlotte pulled a kitchen knife from the fichu at her bosom and plunged it into his heart. It pierced his lung, his aorta, and the left ventricle. He called out to his wife, and died.

Charlotte's escape was prevented by Marat's friends and family, who lived with him. She gave up without a struggle, resigned to sacrificing her life for her ideals, as her ancestor Corneille had preached. At her trial, she testified that she had planned and carried out the assassination alone, with no accomplices. This frustrated the Jacobins, who wanted a good excuse for a mass persecution of Girondists. They ordered her lawyer to plead insanity, which would at least humiliate and discredit her. He couldn't bear it. The best he could come up with were the words, "This incredible calm . . . this complete tranquillity and abnegation which in their way are sublime, are not natural."

At least, if we're to judge from the portrait done of her by a National Guard officer named Hauer, she doesn't seem to have been mistreated in prison. She looks at peace and is even wearing her fashionable mob cap. As payment for the portrait, Charlotte gave the young officer a lock of her hair. Hauer was not the only romantic young man to be moved by this calm, lovely woman. A witness to her execution, Pierre Notelet, wrote, "Her beautiful face was so calm, that one would have said she was a statue. . . . For eight days I was in love with Charlotte Corday."

There were no lengthy appeals, no years spent on Death Row. Four days after Marat's assassination, Charlotte climbed the steps to the guillotine in her dainty little slippers and was beheaded.

Like all assassins, Charlotte naively believed that killing one person would make everything better. Of course, that never happens, and her plan backfired. Instead, Marat became a martyr. Along with David's famous painting, busts of Marat sprang up all over Paris, replacing the crucifixions and Madonnas that were *icons non grata* in the new regime. An obelisk was erected as a memorial to him a month after his death, and at least six plays about the assassination were written and performed. Parents named their children after him, and the names of streets, towns, and bridges were changed. Montmartre became Mont-Marat!

This mania lasted two years. Then, thanks to the volatile political temperament of revolutionary France, Marat fell out of favor. Like statues of Lenin after the fall of Communism, his obelisk was overturned and smashed. Children burned their little Marat dolls, and pamphlets entitled "The Crimes of J. P. Marat" were sold in the marketplace. And finally, Charlotte became the heroine: a beautiful girl who gave her life to rid her country of a monster. Fat lot of good it did her—she was still dead.

~*~*~* The Movie ~*~*~*

1964 saw the debut of a hit Broadway play by Peter Wiess, *The Persecution and Assassination of Jean-Paul Marat as performed by the Inmates of the Asylum of Charenton under the Direction of the Marquis de Sade*. To avoid verbal exhaustion, the title was abbreviated as *Marat/Sade* and made into a movie. It's a good movie if you like ambiguity and experimental theater, but don't take it as gospel. Neither Charlotte Corday nor Marat ever spent any time at Charenton, and they were both dead and decayed at the time of the supposed incident, 1808.

"Die with It in Ye, Frankie!"

I f you grew up in Appalachia, chances are you've heard the legend of Frankie Silver, the first woman to be hung in the state of North Carolina and the inspiration for the song, "Frankie and Johnny"—and everything you heard is wrong.

Except for one thing: Frankie Silver did indeed kill her husband, Charlie Silver, on December 22, 1831.

Frances Stewart was probably about seventeen years old when she married Charlie Silver, who may have been all of eighteen. They'd both been born in log cabins across the ridge from each other in the mountains of Buncombe County, North Carolina. The little cove where she grew up is still known as Stewart's Cove. Charlie built them a little one-room log cabin on some land his father gave him, cutting the trees and hewing the logs himself. For all the vast acreage they owned, the Stewarts and Silvers were poor. Their rocky land was a hard place to raise crops, and they depended for food on what the menfolk could shoot, and what berries and herbs the womenfolk could find in the woods. They had to make anything they needed, and their work was hard. Charlie's younger brother Alfred said about Frankie, "She could card and spin her three yards of cotton a day on a big wheel."

Within a year, Frankie had given birth to a baby girl. By then, her life was probably already miserable. They lived secluded lives, miles from the nearest town, and Charlie had already acquired the habit of leaving his young wife alone for days at a time, while he was off drinking and chasing women. Alone with her baby in a dark, tiny cabin in mid-winter, Frankie must have felt painfully isolated, but it was worse when Charlie came home, drunk and abusive.

Everyone knew that Charlie beat Frankie, and they may not have approved, but wife beating was an accepted practice in those days, in those parts. It was only a question of how *badly* a man might beat his wife. There was an unwritten but accepted law called "the rule of thumb," which said that a man shouldn't beat his wife with a stick that was wider than his thumb. Charlie, it was said, broke the rule of thumb.

On December 23, 1831, Frankie trudged up over the ridge and through the snow to the house where Charlie's family lived. Charlie hadn't been home for days, she told them. Their cabin was cold, she'd burned up all the firewood, and she was taking the baby and going home to her folks. She didn't care if he ever came back again. Charlie's family searched the woods and river for him; maybe he'd fallen through the ice, or been attacked by an animal. Finally, Charlie's father hiked forty miles across the mountains to Tennessee, where there lived a slave who, folks said, could "conjure." The slave was gone, but his master used the con-jure ball, a ball on a string that moved like a pendulum, over a map that Charlie's father had drawn. It stopped right over the crude sketch of Charlie's cabin. That's where to look for Charlie, said the man.

Meanwhile, a neighbor, Jack Collis, explored the abandoned cabin. He noticed that there was an extraordinary amount of ash in the fireplace; Frankie's last fire had consumed a huge amount of wood, and had burned very hot and very long. The ashes were suspiciously greasy. Poking around in the fireplace, he discov-ered bits of human bone. Neighbors pried up the floorboards, and found a puddle of blood "large as a hog's liver."

Next the family and friends searched around outside the house, and found grisly parts of Charlie hidden all over, parts that would-n't burn. In a recently dug hole filled with ashes was the iron heel off one of his hunting shoes. A hollow tree stump concealed his liver and heart. Meanwhile, Charlie's family was burying the body parts as quickly as they were found. When they found more parts, instead of opening the grave, they dug a new grave, with the result that Charlie Silver has three graves.

On January 10, 1832, Burke County Sheriff W. C. Butler arrested Frankie Silver for the murder of her husband. But there was a problem: little Frankie stood four feet, ten inches high. Charlie was big, and weighed twice as much as she. Could she have dragged his body to the fireplace and chopped it up herself? She had to have had help. So along with Frankie, the sheriff arrested Frankie's mother and her brother Blackston. They were quickly let go for lack of evidence, but Frankie was brought to trial, and within two days she was found guilty and sentenced to be hanged by the neck until dead.

The prosecution—and the legend—accused her of hacking up Charlie and burning his pieces out of jealousy for his affairs with various women. Frankie never got to tell her side of the story because she was not allowed to testify. The old English law, under which North Carolina still operated at the time, did not allow accused people to take the witness stand.

However, the ladies of Burke and Buncombe counties seem to have understood. Perhaps they were all too familiar with spousal abuse, which was so accepted that the year Frankie killed her husband, a man went on trial in Burke County for beating his wife to death with a ramrod. He was found guilty and fined $3.60! Perhaps the ladies of Burke and Buncombe counties considered themselves fortunate because their more enlightened husbands didn't break the rule of thumb. In a clemency petition to the governor, signed by thirty-three women, they wrote,

> The neighborhood people are Convinced (sic) that his treatment to her was both unbecoming and cruel very often and at the time too when female Delicacy (sic) would most forbid it. He treated her with personal violence.

The allusion to "female Delicacy" seems to suggest that Charlie beat Frankie while she was pregnant.

Of course, women could not vote or serve on a jury.

On May 18, 1833, a month before she was to be hanged, Frankie escaped. Frankie never told, but the theory was that her brother, a talented whittler, carved a key from wood and opened Frankie's cell door. It took a few days, but the sheriff caught up with her, disguised in boy's clothing, her long hair cropped, following her uncle's wagon on foot. He rode up to the "boy" behind the wagon and asked, "Are you Frankie Silver?"

"No sir," answered Frankie. "My name is Tommy."

And that's when her clueless uncle blew it by turning and answering, from the wagon, "That's right, her name is Tommy."

Back in prison again, and finally resigned to her fate, Frankie dictated a confession, which sadly has been lost. Charlie had come home stinking drunk, she said, and it was worse than before. Maybe Frankie had decided not to accept his harsh treatment any longer, for this time she fought back. Charlie threatened to shoot her and started loading his gun. She grabbed an ax and let him have it. It was plainly a case of self-defense, but all it got for Frankie was a stay of two weeks from the governor, to give Frankie time to "prepare herself" for death.

On July 12, 1833, Frankie Silver mounted the steps to the scaffold. For the past eighteen months, except for that too-brief period of freedom, she had been shackled to the floor of her cell. She was asked if she had any last words. This would be the time for her to reveal what accomplices, if any, she'd had. Her father, standing in the crowd, shouted out, "Die with it in ye, Frankie!"

Frankie said nothing. A good daughter, she took her secret to the gallows.

↬ Frankie Silver is the only woman in this book who left no portrait, but this nineteenth-century drawing could easily be Frankie trudging through the snow with firewood to burn Charlie. Records report that she had long fair hair.

✦✦✦✦✦ What Wasn't True ✦✦✦✦✦

According to the legend—and according to *Ripley's Believe It or Not*—one of those sympathetic ladies of Burke and Buncombe counties had baked a cake for Frankie Silver on the morning she was to be hanged. She asked to be allowed finish the cake, and was granted permission. Frankie ate her cake, brushed the crumbs off her chin, and went to her death.

Frankie and Charlie Silver were definitely not the inspiration for the song "Frankie and Johnny," which stems from a Mississippi Delta black blues tradition. There's another song, though, called "The Ballad of Frankie Silver." Legend has it that Frankie Silver wrote it and sang it on the scaffold before they hung her. Since poor Frankie was illiterate, this is highly unlikely. In the song, Frankie confesses:

> His feeble hands fell gently down,
> His chattering tongue soon lost its sound,
> To see his soul and body part
> It strikes with terror in my heart.
> The jealous thought that first gave strife
> To make me take my husband's life,
> For months and days I spent my time
> Thinking how to commit this crime.

And on a dark and doleful night
I put the body out of sight,
With flames I tried to him consume,
But time would not admit it done.

Frankie wasn't even really the first woman to be hanged in North Carolina, although that's what it says on her grave. At least nine women preceded her either to the gallows or the stake.

The Canadian Conundrum

Today, when you pick up the newspaper, the odds are on any given day you'll find at least one murder reported. In order for such cases even to get headlines, the murders have to be particularly horrendous, or someone famous has to be the victim or perpetrator. So it's hard for today's jaded society to understand why, in 1843, all of Canada was in an uproar over a mere double homicide. One reason was that one of the accused killers was a pretty teenaged girl. The other reason was that both suspects were Irish.

Every society has its scapegoat, some ethnic or racial group that is lowest on its totem pole. In nineteenth-century North America, the scapegoats were the Irish. All during that century, shiploads of poor Irish farmers tried to escape the misery and starvation of their lives in the Old Country by emigrating to Canada and the United States. Once there, they found themselves hardly better off and with few choices. Many people simply would not hire them, and jobs that were advertised in the newspapers often included the warning, "No Irish Need Apply." If they found work at all, it was as servants, working hard jobs that nobody else would take, for less money than anyone else would accept. In return they were reviled and called dishonest, lazy, and stupid. In cartoons of the period, they're drawn to look like monkeys.

Sixteen-year-old Grace Marks was a housemaid. It's almost impossible to imagine how hard housemaids worked in those days. From before sunrise to well after dark, their lives consisted of endless hours spent dusting, scrubbing, cooking, and washing, all before any time-saving appliances existed. If they had a kind master or mistress, they might get a day off on Sunday. Grace Marks had been doing this since she was thirteen, when she arrived in Canada from Ireland along with her father and eight sisters and brothers. Her mother had died on the ship coming over. Conditions in steerage on the emigrant ships were ghastly, with too many people crowded below decks amid rats, filth, and chaos, and it was not uncommon for passengers to die onboard.

In July 1843, Grace had been working for less than a month in the household of Thomas Kinnear, a well-to-do gentleman farmer who owned twenty-five acres outside of the tiny village of Richmond Hill, near Toronto. The only other servants were Nancy Montgomery, the housekeeper, and twenty-year-old James McDermott, the hired man. Like Grace, McDermott was an Irish immigrant. On the last Sunday of the month, two neighbors, suspicious because the house was empty, searched the place and found Kinnear's body in the cellar, shot once through the heart. All three servants were missing, along with some silver, money, various other objects, and Kinnear's horse and carriage.

It took a week more for Nancy Montgomery to be found, badly decomposed, in the hot cellar. She had been killed first, strangled and hit on the head with a heavy object, and hidden behind some tubs. At least one grisly version of the story relates that her body had been cut into four pieces before being hidden beneath a tub. It had been common knowledge that Nancy was sleeping with her master, and sure enough, an autopsy revealed that she was pregnant. The plot thickened.

A manhunt quickly turned up Grace and McDermott staying at the Lewiston Hotel on the United States side of the Niagara River. She had registered under the name of Mary Whitney, and the two were in separate rooms, but the mere fact that she was sleeping under the same roof as a man started tongues wagging: Grace was obviously a hussy, a tart, a piece of baggage, and what could you expect from an Irish immigrant?

It didn't help matters when Grace and McDermott showed up for the inquiry dressed in the clothing of the dead couple, McDermott in Kinnear's waistcoat, Grace in Nancy's best dress and bonnet, and even with a parasol.

The trial of Grace Marks and James McDermott was yet another trial of the century, and was reported in newspapers as far away as London and New York. It had all the elements of sex and violence that the public always finds irresistible. Proper citizens were made uneasy by the thought of servants killing their masters, and were horrified by the accused murderess's youth and her beauty. The only portrait of Grace, drawn at her trial, does indeed show her to have been very pretty, despite her years of drudgery.

Grace's good looks made it easy for people to believe James McDermott when he said she was a vamp who put him under her spell and made him kill. McDermott's story was that neither of them got along particularly well with Nancy, who put on airs and bossed them around, just what you'd expect from someone who's sleeping with the boss. Grace was jealous of Nancy and convinced McDermott to kill her. She had even tried to get him to help poison Nancy's porridge. In fact, he said it was Grace who had strangled Nancy. Grace wanted Kinnear for herself. Trouble was, after killing Nancy and hiding her body, McDermott decided they had to do away with Kinnear, too. When Grace objected, he did it himself.

Grace Marks alias Mary Whitney

↜ The only known drawing of Grace, at her trial

Of course, that's not the way Grace told it. Her version agreed with McDermott on the first and last part—Nancy had indeed been a pain in the butt, and Grace had indeed objected to Kinnear's murder—but she testified that Nancy's murder was also his idea, and that, fearing he might kill her too, she was forced to help him. When the exasperated prosecutor asked why, if she'd been against the killing of Nancy and Kinnear, she had never warned them, why afterward she had packed the household valuables and willingly run off with McDermott, he drew blank stares from little blue-eyed Grace. Well gosh, she'd had to promise McDermott to keep his plot a secret, so how could she tell? Plus he *had* promised to marry her when they got to the United States, so didn't that make it okay? Public opinion was divided on whether she was young and naive and not very bright—after all, everyone *knew* the Irish were stupid!—or whether she was a conniving Jezebel.

Both McDermott and Grace were found guilty, but only McDermott hung. He went to the gallows still insisting it had been Grace's fault. According to the local newspaper:

> The prisoner confessed to the murders, and added . . . when the housekeeper was thrown down the cellar . . . Grace Marks followed him into the cellar and brought a piece of white cloth with her. . . . Grace Marks tied the cloth round her neck and strangled her.

As for Grace, her face turned out to be her fortune, or else people couldn't bring themselves to believe such a sweet child could be guilty of a double murder. At any rate, she was sentenced to life in prison. After a number of years in the Provincial Penitentiary in Kingston, Ontario, some prison official decided she was crazy and got her transferred to the lunatic asylum in Toronto, but by about 1853 she was sane and back in the slammer again. In both institutions, she was the star attraction. Proper ladies and gentlemen used to visit the prisons for entertainment, the way you might visit a zoo or museum. They would request to see the notorious murderess, and Grace would be hauled out and paraded around for them like a two-headed calf at a county fair. One of the people who saw her, both in prison and in the funny farm, was writer Susanna Moodie. In her 1853 book, *Life in the Clearings,* and in the flowery language of the period, she describes crazy Grace,

> lighted up with the fire of insanity, and glowing with a hideous and fiend-like merriment. . . . It appears that even in the wildest bursts of her terrible malady, she is continually haunted by a memory of the past. . . . When will she sit at the feet of Jesus, clothed with the unsullied garments of his righteousness, the stain of blood washed from her hand, and her soul redeemed and pardoned, and in her right mind?

Grace was finally pardoned—by prison officials rather than Jesus—after thirty years in prison. She moved to the United States, changed her name, and was never heard from again, probably much to her relief. But she always stuck to her story that James McDermott had been the bad guy, not she. In 1872, when her pardon was being considered, she was asked, "What has been the general cause of your misfortune and what has been the immediate cause of the crime for which you have been sent to the penitentiary?"

Her answer: "Having been employed in the same house with a villain."

⤖⤖⤖ The Ballad ⤖⤖⤖

Today, when women kill, they get a made-for-TV movie. In those days, they got a ballad:

> Grace Marks she was a serving maid,
> Her age was sixteen years,
> McDermott was a stable hand,
> They worked at Thomas Kinnear's.
>
> Now Thomas Kinnear was a gentleman,
> And a life of ease led he,
> And he did love his housekeeper,
> Called Nancy Montgomery.

O Nancy's no well-born lady,
O Nancy she is no queen,
And yet she goes in satin and silk,
The finest was ever seen.

Now Grace, she loved good Thomas Kinnear,
McDermott he loved Grace,
And 'twas those loves as I do tell
That brought them to disgrace.

O Grace, please be my own true love,
O no it cannot be,
Unless you kill for my dear sake,
Nancy Montgomery.

He struck a blow all with his axe,
On the head of Nancy fair,
He dragged her to the cellar door
And threw her down the stairs.

McDermott held her by the hair,
And Grace Marks by the head,
And these two monstrous criminals,
They strangled her till dead.

Now Thomas Kinnear came riding home,
And on the kitchen floor,

McDermott shot him through the heart
And he weltered in his gore.

All in the middle of the night,
To Toronto they did flee,
Then across the lake to the United States,
Thinking they would scape free.

They had not been in bed six hours,
Six hours or maybe more,
When at the Lewiston hotel there came,
A knock upon the door.

O who is there, said Grace so fair,
What business have you with me?
O you have murdered good Thomas Kinnear,
And Nancy Montgomery.

Young Jamie Walsh stood up in court,
The truth he swore to tell,
O Grace is wearing Nancy's dress,
And Nancy's bonnet as well!

McDermott by the neck they hanged,
Upon the gallows high,
And Grace in prison drear they cast,
Where she must pine and sigh.

Forty Whacks

Actually, Lizzie's father received ten and her step-mother nineteen; a total of only twenty-nine whacks in all, but enough to crush Abby Borden's skull, slice Andrew Borden's eye in half, sever his nose, and render his face into an unrecognizable pulp. And it may not even have been an ax. A hatchet was suggested as the weapon, even a heavy candelabrum. The murder weapon was never found. Plus, Lizzie Borden was found innocent.

In August 1892, maiden lady Lizzie was thirty-two years old and her maiden lady sister Emma was forty. The Borden family lived in a dark, cramped wooden house in a shabby neighborhood in Fall River, Massachusetts. The only running water came from the kitchen sink, and the only toilet was located in the cellar. They didn't even own a horse and buggy.

They could have lived in a better house in a better neighborhood; Andrew Borden was, ironically, a retired undertaker and very rich. He was president of at least two banks, director of at least four companies, and he owned quite a bit of real estate. Fall River's gentry all lived in mansions on "The Hill," the town's exclusive neighborhood, but Andrew was a miser. He was a dour, old bearded guy who didn't socialize much or even attend church. His first wife had died when Lizzie was two years old, and he'd married plain, heavyset Abby because he needed a wife and unpaid housekeeper. Emma and Lizzie refused to call her "Mother."

Each member of the Borden household had their own room, which they kept locked. The front door was secured with not one, but three locks, this in that sweet long-ago time when many people didn't bother to lock their doors at all. Emma and Lizzie didn't even eat with Andrew and Abby, preferring to wait in their respective rooms until their father and stepmother had finished and left the room. Then they would go downstairs and forage the leftovers. It was not a happy household.

Here are some things that had happened before the famous double murder:

Lizzie loved animals and kept a coop of pigeons in their barn. When small boys started breaking into the barn, presumably to get at the pigeons, Andrew Borden's solution was to chop the heads off all the pigeons. At her trial, Lizzie recalled asking her father, "Where are their heads?"

Abby Borden kept a cat, which had learned how to push open doors. One day the cat pushed open the door to Lizzie's room, where she was entertaining guests. Lizzie—the animal lover—

carried the cat downstairs, put its little head on the chopping block, and chopped it off. For days Abby wondered where her cat had gone. Finally Lizzie told her, "You go downstairs and you'll find your cat."

On August 4, 1892, Fall River sweltered under a heat wave, with thermometers hovering around the 100-degree mark. The family had been sick the day before, and Lizzie had expressed fears that they were being poisoned. Abby had even called for the doctor, but tightwad Andrew, not wanting to spend the money, had sent him right back to his office, preferring to self-dose on castor oil. For some reason, nobody suspected the leftover joint of mutton or the warmed-over fish that the family had been consuming for the past week. There was, of course, no refrigerator.

Breakfast early that morning consisted of johnny cakes, cookies, bread, more week-old mutton, and mutton soup. Apparently Andrew and Abby, although they'd spent the night throwing up, managed to get all this down, with the aid of a visiting uncle, John Vinnicum Morse, horse trader by profession. Later Lizzie came downstairs, drank a cup of coffee, and ate a few cookies.

The mutton was starting to work its effects on Bridget, the Irish maid, and she felt queasy, but Abby Borden directed her to wash all the windows that day, heat wave or not. First, however, Bridget went out into the back yard and vomited for fifteen minutes. By the way, even though the maid's name was Bridget, the Borden sisters called her Maggie. That had been the name of their last Irish maid, and, after all, one Irish maid is the same as another, right?

Andrew went out at 9 A.M. to check on one of his businesses. Uncle John Vinnicum was also away on business, presumably trading horses. Emma was away visiting friends. As for Abby, Lizzie told Bridget that her stepmother had received a note and had gone off to see a sick friend.

At around 10:40 A.M. Andrew returned home, carrying a small parcel wrapped in paper. It contained a broken lock that the old skinflint had picked off the floor of one of his properties. He had trouble opening the triple-locked front door of their house, and Bridget had to leave off her window washing to open the door for him. As she stood at the entrance, letting him in, she heard a sound that was very unusual in that house. Lizzie Borden stood at the top of the stairs, laughing out loud.

Bridget didn't know it at the time, but Abby Borden already lay in a pool of blood on the floor of the upstairs guest bedroom.

Like a solicitous daughter, Lizzie helped her father relax on the dark horsehair sofa, so that he could nap in the heat. She pulled off his shoes and folded his coat under his head for a pillow. She then told Bridget about a sale of dress goods at a local shop—to get her out of the house? Bridget said she'd go later, and climbed the stairs to her little attic room to lie down for a while.

She was roused shortly after 11 A.M. by Lizzie's shout, "Maggie, come down! Father's dead!"

Bridget ran for the doctor and for Lizzie's friend Miss Alice Russell; Lizzie called her next-door neighbor, Mrs. Adelaide Churchill; a news dealer named John Cunningham, who heard the row from his shop, was the first person to actually think of calling the police. While he was at it, he called the newspapers. By 11:45, when the police arrived at the Borden house, a crowd had already gathered outside. Inside, the doctor examined the gory remains of Andrew Borden, while in another room, Mrs. Churchill and Miss Russell took turns fanning Lizzie, rubbing her hands, and bathing her forehead.

The doctor asked for a sheet to cover the body. Lizzie answered, "Better get two."

And where was Mrs. Borden, anyway? First Lizzie repeated the story of the note and the sick friend. Then she added, come to think of it, she might have heard her stepmother come in and that maybe she was upstairs. Maybe, in fact, she'd been killed too. Would someone go upstairs and look? Bridget and Mrs. Churchill climbed the stairs and—surprise!—found Abby with her head crushed in, the blood already congealed.

Bodies spoil quickly in hot weather. The funeral was held three days later, and about 4,000 people jammed the streets of Fall River. Abby and Andrew Borden were buried without their heads, which the police had confiscated for evidence. While Emma and Lizzie stood watching their father's coffin being lowered into the grave, the police were at the Borden house, fruitlessly searching Lizzie's closet for a bloodstained dress. The following Thursday, Lizzie was arrested for the murder of her father and stepmother.

Then came the trial. Can you say media circus? Feminist leader Lucy Stone, the suffragettes, and the Women's Christian Temperance Union all filled reams of paper with petitions to free Lizzie, who for some reason became a feminist cause. Journalists from all over the world fought their way into the courtroom. Lizzie was tried, not by a jury of her peers, because women couldn't serve on juries, but by a jury of her father's peers: twelve bearded old guys.

And some interesting facts emerged:

Where had Lizzie been while her father was being butchered? In the hayloft of the barn, said Lizzie, where her massacred pigeons had once lived, looking for a metal sinker for her fishing line, and then eating a pear. But a policeman who'd climbed up to the loft testified that a thick layer of undisturbed dust covered the floor.

Miss Russell testified that on Sunday, August 7, she saw Lizzie burning a light blue dress at the stove. It was just an old thing, covered with paint, Lizzie had explained.

So what had she been wearing on the morning of the murders? Lizzie produced a dark blue silk dress. A fancy silk dress to hang around the house in, climb up to a dusty loft in? I don't think so, and neither did most everyone else.

A druggist testified that on the day before the murders, Lizzie had tried to buy 10 cents worth of prussic acid from him, to kill insects on her sealskin cape, she said. Well, if she couldn't buy poison and if the mutton wouldn't do the job, an ax might have to serve.

That note about the sick friend, delivered to Abby? It was never found.

During the trial, Lizzie's lawyer kept referring to his thirty-two-year-old client as "this poor defenseless girl," even as "this poor *orphan* girl." At first Lizzie was cool and collected, and her testimony was pretty snide.

↪ Lizzie faints in court. From a nineteenth-century newspaper report of the trial.

QUESTION: Why did you leave off calling (Abby Borden) mother?

LIZZIE: Because I wanted to.

But she soon commenced weeping and fainting during the trial, like the public expected a woman to act. In the stifling court-room, in those days without air conditioning, you might faint, too, dressed like Lizzie was: a high-necked, long-sleeved black dress trimmed with velvet, a straw poke bonnet, and black cotton gloves.

Lizzie was dressed like a lady. For Lizzie Borden *was* an upstanding lady, and the jury couldn't bring themselves to convict her. They acquitted her on the first ballot and then sat around for an hour more before returning to the courtroom, or it wouldn't have looked right.

After the trial, Lizzie and Emma, now rich, bought themselves a nice fourteen-room mansion on The Hill, along with a horse and carriage. Lizzie changed her name to Lizbeth. It was all too late. Lizzie had gotten away with murder, and the gentry, although they didn't want one of their own hanged, also didn't care to socialize with her. The sisters lived in seclusion, until Lizzie started hanging out with theater people in Boston, particularly an actress named Nance O'Neill, who came up to the mansion to visit. Lizzie threw big parties for Nance and her theater pals. Shocked by this unseemly bohemian—and perhaps lesbian?—behavior, Emma moved out. The sisters never spoke to each other again.

Lizzie died in 1927 and Emma followed her to the grave nine days later. In her will, Lizzie, the animal lover, the cat killer, left $30,000 to the Fall River Animal Rescue League.

Scores of books, plays, operas, and a ballet have been written about Lizzie and her hatchet, with enough theories advanced to put Kennedy assassination theorists to shame. The maid did it, Uncle Vinnicum did it, a raving maniac did it. My favorite adaptation of Lizzie's story is Agnes DeMille's beautiful ballet, *Fall River Legend.* DeMille, deciding that an acquittal isn't very visually interesting onstage, changed the ending and had Lizzie hung.

✢✢✢✢ That Jingle ✢✢✢✢

The famous rhyme, already being chanted by children before Lizzie's trial had even started, was sung to the tune of the then-popular song, "Tarara Boom De-Ay":

> Lizzie Borden took an ax
> And gave her mother forty whacks.
> When she saw what she had done,
> She gave her father forty-one.

But why forty-one? Why not twenty-one, or fifty-one? We'll never know, because the person or persons who wrote this immortal jingle are lost in the mists of time.

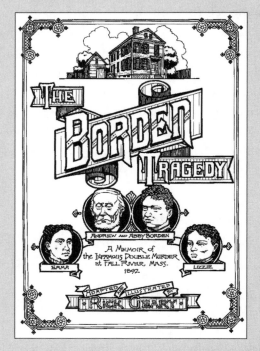

↬ The Borden house and the main characters, from Rick Geary's graphic novel *The Borden Tragedy*

Shoots Like a Girl: Women Who Missed

"I Came Here to Die"

On a rainy March 1, 1954, four Puerto Rican nationalists ascended the steps of the House of Representatives in Washington D.C. They had bought one-way train tickets from New York City because they knew they would not return. Their leader was a stunningly beautiful woman, fashionably attired in a suit and high-heeled patent leather shoes, a chic silk scarf tied around her neck. Her name was Lolita Lebron.

Passing the front-door guard, whose only concern was whether they were carrying cameras, they took seats in the balcony. On the floor, 243 house members were debating a law concerning Mexican farm workers. Lolita stood and walked down the aisle, wrapping herself in the Puerto Rican flag that she had brought with her. The three men Rafael Cancel Miranda, Andres Figueroa Cordero, and Irving Flores Rodriguez followed her. At the front of the balcony, she held up a pistol with both hands, shouted, "Freedom for Puerto Rico! Independencia!" and started shooting. Behind her, Miranda, Cordero, and Rodriguez followed her lead, spraying the chamber with twenty to twenty-five rounds of bullets.

Bullets ricocheted off the walls and ceiling—some of the bullet holes can still be seen today—and when it was over, five congressmen lay wounded: George Fallon of Maryland, shot in the hip; Clifford Davis of Tennessee and Kenneth Roberts of Alabama, both hit in the leg; Ben Jensen of Iowa, struck in the shoulder; and Alvin Bentley of Michigan, the most badly wounded, shot in the chest, the bullet puncturing his lung, liver, and stomach. All survived.

↭ Lolita, under arrest

The four Puerto Ricans were immediately taken into custody—they didn't resist. Actually, they had expected to be shot down by the guards. In her purse Lolita carried a letter, which read in part: "My life I give for the freedom of my country. . . . I take responsibility for everything." She told reporters, "I am not sorry for what I did. . . . In future centuries, people will understand."

Puerto Rico, which had been a Spanish colony (nobody asked the Puerto Ricans whether they wanted to belong to Spain), was ceded to the United States in 1898, after the Spanish-American War (nobody asked the Puerto Ricans whether they wanted to belong to the United States). In 1952 the little island, about half the size of New Jersey, became a commonwealth of the United States. Puerto Rican citizens can be drafted into war by the United States, but they can't vote for a president.

This was not the first act of violence on the part of Puerto Rican nationalists. In 1950, Griselio Torresola and Oscar Collazo attempted to assassinate Harry Truman. They managed to wound two guards and kill one before bullets stopped them, killing Torresola and wounding Collazo. But Lolita, Miranda, Cordero, and Rodriguez didn't have death on their minds when they shot up Congress; they simply wanted to draw attention to their cause. As Lolita declared, "I did not come here to kill. I came here to die."

Born in Puerto Rico in 1919, Lolita grew up in a small house near the coffee plantation where her father worked as foreman. The Lebron family was better off than most. Many poor Puerto Rican farmers had lost their land to the big plantation owners and had no alternative but to work planting and harvesting Puerto Rico's main crops, sugar and coffee. Lolita grew into a beautiful teenager whose village crowned her Queen of the Flowers of May at the age of seventeen, but she never got beyond eighth grade. By 1939, at the age of twenty, she'd given birth to a baby girl, whose father did not stick around. In 1941, leaving her baby with her parents, Lolita sailed for New York City, the land of opportunity.

In New York, Lolita found work in a sewing machine factory. She married, gave birth to a son, and divorced. She also became radicalized, joining the Puerto Rican Nationalist Party. She grew more and more dedicated to Puerto Rico's liberation and became president of an organization called Puerto Rican Women for Liberty. By this point, the FBI was keeping tabs on the Nationalist Party and had a file on Lolita. They went so far as to check up on her at her workplace, but for all their efforts remained clueless about the planned shooting.

At Lolita's trial, in July 1954, she sat quietly and read her Bible during the proceedings. There was a side of Christian mysticism to Lolita that one doesn't expect to find in revolutionaries. She

↬ This mural of Lolita adorns a wall on East 109th Street in New York's Harlem

and her companions were sentenced to seventy-five years in prison for conspiracy to overthrow the government of the United States, and in prison, Lolita began to get mystic religious visions. That was all the excuse that the authorities needed to get her transferred to St. Elizabeth's psychiatric hospital in 1957. As with Charlotte Corday, Grace Marks, and Winnie Ruth Judd, the men in authority seemed to be more comfortable believing that if a woman was violent, she must be crazy. Lolita spent nine months in St. Elizabeth's before returning to prison.

Lolita Lebron and her companions were pardoned by Jimmy Carter in 1979. By that time, she had become a national heroine in her country. When, in 1977, she was briefly allowed out of prison to attend her daughter's funeral in Puerto Rico, people lined the streets, waiting to catch a glimpse of their idol, chanting, "Lolita, Lolita, Lolita!"

↜↜ Old Revolutionaries Don't Fade Away ↝↝

Release from prison in 1979 didn't put an end to Lolita the radical. She continues to work for Puerto Rican independence and still doesn't hesitate to break the law for what she considers a sacred cause. On May 4, 2000, 102 years after the United States annexed Puerto Rico, the eighty-year-old revolutionary heroine was arrested, along with other protesters, at a nonviolent demonstration on the Puerto Rican island of Vieques. The tiny island, four kilometers long and three kilometers wide, occupied by the American military since 1940, is used for bombing practice and simulated war games. The demonstrations had started in 1999, after security guard Davis Sanes was killed and four others were wounded when two 500-pound bombs missed their target and instead hit the observation tower where Sanes was employed.

↜ Lolita, today

While awaiting the U.S. marshals and FBI agents who were coming to arrest her and the other protesters, Lolita commented, "I just hope the Americans don't keep an old lady like me waiting too long in this heat."

"I Am a Flower Child"

For those who'd like to know how not to become a killer, research has shown this much: Don't get abused as a child, and don't quit school or leave home at sixteen to marry or have a baby. Actually, Valerie Jean Solanas did the statistics one better: she left home at fifteen and got herself pregnant by a sailor. It's not known whether she had the baby or not, but certainly by 1966, when she wound up in Greenwich Village, she was alone. True to form, she had been sexually molested by her father, who deserted the family in the 1940s, and was whipped by her grandfather when she refused to stay in Catholic school.

Miraculously, Valerie managed to graduate high school, go on to do well at the University of Maryland, and even pursue a year of graduate studies at the University of Minnesota. During all this time, she supported herself by prostitution. By the time she got to Greenwich Village, Valerie had become a lesbian, but prostitution continued to keep her alive, along with panhandling and selling mimeographed copies of her newly written *SCUM Manifesto* on the streets. The *SCUM* (it stands for Society for Cutting

Up Men, and the only member of the Society was Valerie) *Manifesto* is an angry and funny declaration of extremely radical second-wave feminism. Feminist writers have called it everything from "a sacred text" (Roxanne Dunbar) to "the fulmination of a sadly disturbed woman" (Susan Brownmiller). Valerie's first paragraph sums the rest of the book up nicely:

> Life in this society being, at best, an utter bore and no aspect of society being at all relevant to women, there remains to civic-minded, responsible, thrill-seeking females only to overthrow the government, eliminate the money system, institute complete automation and destroy the male sex.

Haven't *you* felt like that every now and then?

Andy Warhol was a pop-art superstar and a starmaker. He invented the word *superstar.* In his "Factory," a grimy, silver-walled office in downtown Manhattan, he mass-produced pop art silkscreens of other superstars: Marilyn Monroe, James Dean, and others. Actually, he didn't even do the original art: the images were taken from photographs, and the work of silkscreening was done by assistants. It didn't matter, as long as he signed them.

He also made dreadful, amateurish films that the art critics adored, in which he starred various hangers-on, all of who were underpaid but grateful to bask in Andy's limelight. Valerie, gaunt and ragged, was a nobody who lived hand-to-mouth and was often homeless. She wanted desperately to be somebody. She saw Andy, his Factory, and his "beautiful people" as her ticket to stardom, and started hanging out there when Andy would let her. He was often bitchy to her, and his wretched crew of transvestites, druggies, losers, and fag-hags were worse. The beautiful Viva (really Susan Hoffman, of Syracuse, New York), one of Andy's superstar brigade, once screamed at Valerie in a crowded restaurant, "You dyke! You're disgusting!" Andy himself once described her as a "hot water bottle with tits," whatever *that* means.

Early in 1967, Valerie gave him a copy of play she'd written, hoping he'd produce it. The play, titled *Up Your Ass,* was so dirty that Andy suspected she might be an undercover cop trying to entrap him. He promptly misplaced it somewhere in the chaos of the Factory, and when Valerie asked for its return that May, he told her he'd lost it. To placate her, he gave her a small part in his film *I, a Man* and paid her all of $25. A review in the *American Film Institute Catalogue of Motion Pictures* describes Valerie as being "the only good thing about that movie."

At the same time, Valerie sold her *SCUM Manifesto* to Olympia Press publisher Maurice Girodias, a Frenchman who had already made a name for himself by publishing edgy books like *Lolita, Candy,* and *Tropic of Cancer.* He gave her the grand sum of $500, which, even in those days, was pretty pathetic. A year later, he was able to pay writer Mary Sativa $2,000 for her hippie cult classic

Acid Temple Ball, so obviously he had the money and could have paid
Valerie more. In an interview with me, Sativa remembered
Girodias as being "elegant and charming," and he seems to have
used that charm to get Valerie to sign a contract she later regret-
ted. According to actor, filmmaker, and Warhol associate Paul
Morrisey, the contract said something like, "I will give you five
hundred dollars and you will give me your next writing and other
writings." Valerie interpreted this to mean that Girodias would
own everything that she wrote for the rest of her life.

Despite Morrisey's reassurance that the contract wasn't worth
the paper it was written on, she panicked. First Andy had stolen
Up Your Ass (she thought), and now Maurice Girodias was stealing
everything else she would ever write. In a fit of paranoia, Valerie
decided that the two of them were in it together, plotting to steal
her life's work. (Ironically, Andy and Girodias didn't even *know*
each other!)

Valerie began to harass Girodias. In his introduction to the
1968 Olympia Press first edition of *The SCUM Manifesto,* the publisher writes:

> Obviously, the pixies were moving in, pretty fast. She
> started calling me, day and night, either to insult me, or
> to ask me in an urgent voice what I thought of her. . . .
> Further threats, insults and twisted blandishments arrived

by mail, sometimes in envelopes addressed to "Girodias-the-Toad."

She approached Paul Krassner, publisher of the underground newspaper *The Realist,* and borrowed $50, for food, he believed. With the money she bought a Saturday night special. She had decided to shoot Maurice Girodias. Mary Sativa commented, "I think there must have been a large number of writers who wanted to shoot (Girodias)."

At 9 A.M., on June 3, 1968, Valerie went to the Chelsea Hotel, where Maurice Girodias lived, only to learn that he was gone for the weekend. She waited there for three hours and finally made her way to the Factory, where Paul Morrisey found her waiting outside for Andy Warhol. Andy wasn't coming in that day, he told her. "Well that's alright, I'll wait," Valerie answered. And wait she did. Finally, at 4 P.M., Andy showed up, and they came up in the elevator together. Valerie was actually pretty that day; she had put on makeup, dressed for the part, and for a change was not wearing her Bob Dylan cap. She'd been prepared to shoot Girodias, but if he was unavailable, Andy would have to do. But Andy didn't know that when he commented, "Look, doesn't Valerie look good?"

As they emerged from the elevator, the phone was ringing. It was Viva, for Andy. She hoped to worm some money out of him to pay her electric bill before they shut off her power. As Andy spoke to Viva, Valerie took a .32 automatic pistol from the brown paper bag she had tucked under her arm, and shot him once, twice, both shots missing him. Her third bullet penetrated his lungs, spleen, liver, and esophagus. Andy fell to the floor, and she turned her gun on Mario Amaya, an art critic who'd been waiting to meet Andy. She got him in the right hip, and he limped to safety in the back studio, locking the door behind him. Fred Hughes, Andy's manager, was next. Valerie aimed her gun at his head—and the elevator door opened! Drawing on God only knows what reserves of strength and nerve, Hughes said, "Oh, there's the elevator. Why don't you get on, Valerie?"

↬ Valerie, from the cover of her *SCUM Manifesto*

And she did!

At 8 P.M. that night, Valerie turned herself in to a cop who was directing traffic in Times Square. She gave her reason for shooting Andy: "He had too much control of my life." Inexplicably she added, "I am a flower child." A judge sent her to the psych ward.

The feminists adored her! Radical feminist lawyer Flo Kennedy, who defended her, said she was "one of the most important spokeswomen of the feminist movement." Ti Grace Atkinson, New York chapter president of NOW, called her, "the first outstanding champion of women's rights." Robin Morgan's 1970 feminist diatribe against the male-dominated left wing, *Good-bye to All That,* ends with the declaration: "FREE VALERIE SOLANAS! FREE OUR SISTERS! FREE OURSELVES!"

On Christmas Eve 1968, Valerie actually phoned Andy at the Factory, demanding he pay $20,000 for her lost manuscript, so she could use the money for her defense. Needless to say, she didn't get the money. Andy did, however, refuse to testify against her, and in June 1969, she was given three years for "reckless assault with intent to harm." The year she'd spent in the psych ward counted as time served. Velvet Underground superstar Lou Reed commented, "You get more for stealing a car," and wrote a song about it called "I Believe," in which he said that he would have pulled the switch himself to electrocute Valerie.

Andy recovered, but he was never quite the same. An entry in his journal, dated August 7, 1977, reads:

> By the way, Valerie has been seen hanging around the Village and last week when I was cruising there with Victor, I was scared I'd run into her and that would be a really weird thing. What would happen? Would she want to shoot me again?

In 1987, doctors did what Valerie failed to do, and Andy Warhol died in the hospital from a botched gallstone operation. At his funeral in Saint Patrick's Cathedral, an unidentified woman stood outside on the steps and shouted, "The monster is dead! The monster is finally dead!"

Valerie outlived Andy by a year, dying alone at the age of fifty-two, of emphysema and pneumonia, in a cheap San Francisco hotel room. She was still working as a prostitute, and according to her sister sex workers, stayed elegant and slim until the end, dressing in silver lamé.

Valerie's mother, Dorothy Moran, said, "She had a terrific sense of humor."

❦❦❦❦❦ The Movie and the Play ❦❦❦❦❦

In 1996, Lili Taylor played Valerie Solanas in writer-director Mary Harron's *I Shot Andy Warhol*. The film is an excellent reflection of the bizarre life in and around Warhol's Factory, and Taylor is a believable, funny, and poignant Solanas.

Valerie's play *Up Your Ass* was finally discovered in the Warhol Museum, in a box beneath some film lighting equipment, and was produced by the George Coates Performance Works in San Francisco in 2000. The play's lead character, panhandler Bongi Perez—obviously Valerie's alter ego—spouts rage-filled, hilarious, and raunchy invective right out of the author's now world-famous manifesto. As for the *SCUM Manifesto* itself, it can be found on the Internet, on dozens of Web sites.

↜ Valerie Solanas paper dolls, from *Real Girl* comics

"If It Didn't Go Off"

It was 1975, and among the crowd waiting to catch a glimpse of President Gerald Ford that September morning in Sacramento, California, was a slight woman in a long red dress. Some people may have been annoyed at the way she pushed her way to the front of the onlookers; others may have heard her mutter, "He's not your public servant." Some may have even thought the little redhead was kinda cute. Beneath the red dress, she had a Colt .45 automatic strapped to her leg, and she had come to shoot the president. Her name was Squeaky Fromme.

Lynette Alice Fromme seemed like a girl Beaver Cleaver. Growing up during the '50s in an affluent southern California neighborhood, she was cute as a button, with her red hair and freckles. She was an A- student and star of a kids' dance troupe, the Lariats. The troupe traveled all over the country, even visiting the White House and performing on *The Lawrence Welk Show*. Her 1963 graduating class at Orville Wright Junior High named her Personality Plus.

But there are no real-life Beaver Cleavers. Lynette's home life was miserable. Her father was mean and brutal, a control freak. Although he made good money as an aircraft engineer and owned two cars, he would check the odometer after allowing his wife to use the car, to make sure that she hadn't driven further than he authorized, and he took the car keys with him when he went away on business trips. When Lynette entered high school, she had to drop out of her beloved Lariats. She couldn't get to practice sessions because Mr. Fromme would no longer allow his wife to drive her there. She had a sister and brother, but Mr. Fromme seemed to pick on Lynette most often, and sometimes she came to school with makeup covering bruises and black eyes.

As Lynette matured, her father's treatment of her worsened. Several times he kicked her out of their house, announcing, "You're not part of this family anymore." Lynette took minimum wage jobs at hamburger stands and stayed on friends' couches until he let her back. When she turned eighteen, Mr. Fromme kicked his daughter out one last time. She gathered up her meager possessions and hitchhiked to Venice Beach. Sitting on a bench in the sun, wondering where to go, she met Charlie Manson.

Already in his thirties, Charlie had spent most of his life in prison for various petty crimes. His mother, who gave birth to him at sixteen, was jailed for armed robbery when he was five. He lived with his aunt and an uncle whose idea of punishing little Charlie was to make him wear girls' clothes. By the time he was a

teenager, he'd been in too many reformatories and had escaped
from them eighteen times. He had never really learned to read.

Between prison terms, Charlie pimped and fathered at least
two babies with two different women. In prison, he learned to
play guitar. From his cellmates he picked up bits and pieces of
philosophies, from Scientology to Robert Heinlein's hippie classic *Stranger in a Strange Land.* Then in 1967, he was let out of prison
into a brave new world full of big-eyed young people—especially
young *women*—who were looking for a meaning to life. Charlie
used his pimping talents and soon moved in with a pretty twenty-
three-year-old from Berkeley. They hung around Telegraph
Avenue and the Haight-Ashbury with the other hippies, and
Charlie made a little money playing guitar in local clubs. Then
one day he decided to hitchhike to Venice Beach, which he'd
heard was a Southern California version of the Haight, and there
was Lynette.

Now let's call her Squeaky, the nickname she earned as part
of the Manson Family because of her cute little voice. Family was
what both Squeaky and Charlie were looking for. Squeaky wanted
a loving father, and Charlie, who wanted *any* kind of family because
he'd never had one, filled the bill. She became the second of
Charlie's Girls, but he soon acquired more; impressionable
middle-class chicks with long hair and long legs, hanging onto
every word of his pseudo-hippie philosophy, and of course,

sleeping with him. Attracted by the drugs and free sex, young men came along, too, although never as many of them. They drove around California in an old school bus, but most of the time they lived at the Spahn ranch in the southern California desert. The ranch had been used by film studios for decades as a backdrop for Westerns. Owner George Spahn, eighty years old and nearly blind, let the Family crash there for free. It helped that the girls slept with him.

At first, life at the Spahn ranch was comparatively idyllic, if you could accept Charlie's odd philosophy. Vegetarians, the girls dumpster-dived outside of supermarkets for slightly squished fruits and veggies. Charlie was into being, like, natural. Everyone grew their hair long, and the men had beards. Acid flowed freely and it was all about, like, *love,* man.

Like a zillion other Americans, Charlie adored the Beatles and played their *White Album* over and over. In the songs, he heard messages from the Beatles. Songs like "Helter Skelter" and "Little Piggies" told him how big corporations were polluting the Earth, and how there'd be an apocalypse when downtrodden black people, led by the Black Panthers, rose up and destroyed the white. But the Family would be safe, because they'd find the hole in the Mojave Desert that led to an underground paradise where the Aztec king Montezuma had taken his people 500 years ago.

Things went from weird to worse. Motorcycle gangs started

hanging out at the ranch, and the drugs of choice went from acid and pot to speed and heroin. A Family member, Bobby Beausoleil, sold a batch of bad mescaline to some bikers. When they wanted their $2,000 back, Bobby went to the guy he'd bought the mescaline from, a music teacher named Gary Hinman. There was a fight, and Bobby stabbed Gary. Charlie's angels ministered to the poor guy, but three days later he died anyway, and Charlie got a brilliant idea: Let's blame the killing on the Black Panthers. So they wrote "Political Piggy" on the living room wall, in Gary's blood, and left a bloody panther paw print. They also took Gary's Fiat, and Bobby Beausoleil was sleeping in it on the highway when the cops found him and arrested him on suspicion of murder.

↜ Squeaky in her red robes

This was when Charlie got *another* brilliant idea: If they could pin the murder on the Black Panthers, the cops would let Bobby go. Why not kill some more people, anybody would do, and make it look like the Black Panthers did it? And that's what they did.

On August 8, 1969, Charlie sent three girls and one of the

guys, Tex Watson, to a Bel-Air house, where they slaughtered coffee heiress Abigail Folger; her boyfriend Voytek Frykowski; hairstylist Jay Sebring; and Steven Parent, a teenager who was just in the wrong place at the wrong time. The victim who caught the attention of the public, however, was beautiful blonde Sharon Tate, starlet and wife of director Roman Polanski, eight months pregnant with their child.

One of the girls, Sadie Glutz, really Susan Atkins, wrote the word "Pig" on the door in Sharon Tate's blood.

The next day, Charlie came along for the ride, when they invaded the home of Rosemary and Leno LaBianca. But he stayed only long enough to tie up the couple, and left before the killing started. His girls wrote "Death to Pigs" and "War" on the wall in the couple's blood, and on the refrigerator, "Healter" (sic) "Skelter."

A true pimp, Charlie got his girls to commit murder for him and thought he'd kept his hands clean. But Sadie Glutz had talked to Bobby Beausoleil's girlfriend about the killings, and she went to the cops. They busted Sadie, and she talked some more. Soon Tex and the three other girls—and Charlie—were in jail.

But not Squeaky. She was kind of second in command, a den mother to the Family, and Charlie felt she was too important to risk, so he never sent her out to kill. In fact, the ones who killed for Charlie were those followers whom he callously considered expendable. If they were caught, or even killed by the cops, it wouldn't have mattered to him.

With Charlie in jail, Squeaky became the group's leader. During the trial, she and the other girls carved the letter *X* into their foreheads, shaved their heads, and literally moved to the corner of Broadway and Temple Street, just outside the Los Angeles Hall of Justice. They swept the area clean, curled up in the bushes at night, and passed the day singing and giving out statements to the press. As for the press, they loved Squeaky. Not only was she the most verbal, but she was so darned *cute,* with her red hair and freckles!

On January 25, 1971, Charlie and his codefendants were found guilty of murder. After they were sentenced to prison for life, the girls dispersed. They found other boyfriends, mostly hard drug-using motorcycle gang members. Only Squeaky and a few others remained fiercely faithful to Charlie. Squeaky kept up a regular correspondence with him, and she tried to keep the faith, but in her hands Charlie's original mission altered subtly. The war between blacks and whites, the hole in the Mojave Desert, took a back seat to ecology. Ending pollution, stopping the slaughter of whales and baby seals became of utmost importance. She exchanged her embroidered hippie dresses for red robes. Red, she told reporters, was "the blood of sacrifice."

Inspired by the Symbionese Liberation Army, which had

kidnapped newspaper heiress Patty Hearst, Squeaky invented an organization, the International People's Court of Retribution, which existed only in her head. In the name of the People's Court, Squeaky and a few of the last still-faithful girls sent out hundreds of threatening letters to the CEOs of major corporations. Stop polluting or die, they wrote, stop the slaughter of whales and baby seals or we'll slaughter you and your families.

Charlie was moved to Folsom Prison, and Squeaky moved to Sacramento to be near him, bringing the People's Court with her. She was growing more and more fixated on ecology; it was all she wanted to talk about. The people in power were killing trees and animals, destroying the Earth. They must be stopped at all costs!

That's when President Gerald Ford came to visit Sacramento. It was all over the newspapers and the television screens; maps showed where and when he'd be appearing in public. Squeaky developed a plan so loony it could compete with Charlie's plans: She could call attention to Charlie again—he'd been out of the news for some time now—*and* call attention to the disastrous state of the planet at the same time.

On September 5, 1975, Squeaky Fromme strapped her gun, an antique .45, to her leg, hiding it beneath the folds of her long red robe, and joined the crowds in front of the Sacramento Hotel, from which Ford would emerge at 9:55 A.M., on his way to a meet-

ing with Gov. Jerry Brown. Right on time, Ford, flanked by photographers and Secret Service agents, walked out, shaking hands
right and left. And suddenly in front of him was a cute little elfin
redhead in a red robe, with her hand out, but there was a gun in
it, pointed at him. Then Squeaky was on the ground, in the grip
of Secret Service men, her gun wrestled from her hand. "Easy,
boys," witnesses heard her tell them, "it didn't go off." At least one
witness insisted that what she had said was, "It wasn't loaded
anyway."

Indeed, there was no bullet in the gun's chamber.

Days later, Squeaky's public defender would ask her why she did
it. She answered, "For the trees."

⤖⤖⤖ Ford's Problem ⤖⤖⤖

Poor Gerald Ford! An accidental president, he ascended to the
highest office in America first because of the resignation of scandal-clouded Vice President Spiro Agnew, then the resignation of
scandal-clouded Richard Nixon. Never universally hated the way
Nixon and Lyndon Johnson had been, he was a comparatively
bland president, as Republicans go, with a reputation for being
intellectually challenged and even a trifle goofy. He had a habit

of falling down, and it was said that he could not chew gum and walk at the same time.

So why did women keep trying to kill him? Not three weeks after Squeaky Fromme aimed her unloaded .45 at him, again in California—this time San Francisco—a dumpy middle-aged woman named Sarah Jane Moore tried it again, with a .38-caliber revolver. Sarah was a kind of flaky double agent, who hung with various radical groups and informed on them to the FBI. Then she informed on the FBI to her radical pals.

She managed to get off one shot before a bystander knocked the gun away, but missed the president by five feet. "I'm no Squeaky Fromme," she insisted, as they dragged her off. The reason for her attempt, she said, was to "make a statement."

Years later, Bill Clinton, jokingly complaining that no one had ever tried to shoot him, said, "Even Ford had Squeaky Fromme."

The Long Island Lolita

There must be *something* you could say in Amy Fisher's defense. Like, didn't we all do really stupid things when we were seventeen years old that we're now sorry about? Well yeah, but most of us did *not* shoot the wife of the thirty-eight-year-old guy we were having sex with.

Little Amy was a Jewish American, Italian American princess. Her parents owned a prosperous upholstery business, and she grew up in a ranch-style Long Island house, filled with sunshine, pets, and all the toys she wanted. She had a dog named Muffin and her own phone. She was her parents' darling only child.

But life wasn't so perfect after all. It probably didn't make her life much happier when, at the age of twelve, she was raped by the man her father had hired to retile their bathroom. Amy never told anyone, least of all her father. Years later, she would say that her twice-divorced father was a violent man, and that prison was a welcome relief from home life. "People aren't hitting me here," Amy said in her prison cell. "And I'm able to grow."

For Amy's sixteenth birthday her doting parents bought her a used white Dodge, and she managed to total it in less than a year. Daddy took the car—and Amy—to Complete Auto Body and Fender Repair to see if it could be fixed, and that's where Amy met Joey Buttafuoco. Joey's dad owned the company and Joey supervised the mechanics.

He was married to Mary Jo Buttafuoco and had two kids. He was thirty-four years old. And before Amy had turned seventeen, he was in bed with her.

They had sex at motels, where Joey would rent a room by the hour, or in an upstairs room at Complete Auto, or even in Amy's bedroom, before her parents got home from the shop. Or they'd go off together on Joey's boat, aptly named *Double Trouble*. She was still attending high school.

Amy liked older guys; even in ninth grade, she'd ignored the boys in her class in favor of eleventh graders. Joey didn't worry about the fact that he was more than twice her age. He was having the time of his life with a hot teenager. What Amy saw in Joey is another matter. The guy is no Adonis. He's a big, beefy Italian auto repairman with a flattened nose and a heavy Long Island accent. Say! You don't suppose she was looking for a loving father, one who didn't hit her?

About six weeks after she started going to bed with Joey, Amy went to work for the ABBA escort service, a thinly veiled Nassau County prostitution ring, where she averaged $150 for forty-five minutes of sex. She later insisted that it was Joey who pimped her to ABBA. Whatever the truth, owners of another "escort service" would appear on television, along with a prostitute, to say that Joey had been selling cocaine to prostitutes and their pimps, and had been a driver for ABBA, driving the girls to and from their dates, often demanding sex from them in exchange. They called him "Joey Coco Pops."

At ABBA, Amy said she was twenty-one and gave a phony last name. She got herself a steady clientele of rich businessmen, and after about six months, dumped ABBA, took her clients with her, and set herself up as a freelancer. She bragged about it to her friends at John F. Kennedy High School.

She also started having sex with Paul Makely, the twenty-nine-year-old owner of the gym where she and Joey worked out. Then she started having sex with Chris Drellos, an old boyfriend from her pre-Joey days. But she told them both that the only man she really loved was Joey. They didn't care. The sex was great.

Meanwhile, Amy was getting more and more impatient with Joey. It seemed that all he ever wanted was sex. He insisted he loved her, but he wouldn't leave his wife for her. They'd been childhood sweethearts, he told Amy, he could never hurt her.

But what if something should happen to Mary Jo? Amy wondered.

She asked Chris to get her a gun; she wanted to shoot Mary Jo Buttafuoco. Chris couldn't believe it! He tried to stall her; he didn't want to lose the good sex. Anyway, he owed her money. But Amy wouldn't be put off, so in desperation, Chris introduced her to a friend, twenty-one-year-old Stephen Sleeman, who had a .22-caliber rifle. Amy asked him if he'd shoot Mary Jo for her. He said, "Sure."

He just wanted to get laid.

Stephen led Amy on as long as he could, even sawing off the barrel of his shotgun for her when she asked him to and stalking Mary Jo. In return, she gave him blowjobs in his car. But when it became clear to her that Stephen had no intention of shooting anyone, he was yesterday's news. Amy finally got her gun from a Brooklyn College dropout named Peter Guagenti, paying him $800 for it. Oh yeah, and she promised him sex.

On May 19, 1992, Amy went to the high school nurse's office. She felt sick, she explained, she had cramps. She needed to go home early. The nurse excused her from school. Peter Guagenti picked her up in his maroon 1983 Thunderbird and handed her a .25-caliber gun. He drove her to the Buttafuoco house, parked, and waited for her.

Mary Jo was painting some lawn furniture. She came to the

door when Amy rang the bell, and here, according to two books, three made-for-TV movies, and one Internet source, is the gist of their conversation:

AMY: Are you Mrs. Buttafuoco?

MARY JO: Yeah.

AMY: I want to talk to you about your husband, Joey.

MARY JO: What's this about?

AMY: It's not every day that I confront a wife, but your husband, Joey, is having an affair with my sixteen-year-old sister.

MARY JO: Really?

AMY: I think the idea of a forty-year-old man sleeping with a sixteen-year-old girl is disgusting.

MARY JO: Well, he's not forty yet. What's your name?

AMY: Anne Marie.

MARY JO: Where do you live, Anne?

AMY: Over there in Bar Harbor.

MARY JO: Honey, Bar Harbor is in the other direction. Where do you really live?

AMY: On Dolphin Court.

MARY JO: Who's that with you in the car?

AMY: My boyfriend.

MARY JO: What are you trying to pull here?

AMY: Look, I have proof. (And she hands Mary Jo a T-shirt that says, "Complete Auto Body and Fender Repair.")

MARY JO: This isn't even Joey's size. He gives those shirts to a lot of people. Listen, I'm going to go in and call Joey now. Thanks for coming by. (Mary Jo turns to go and Amy shoots her in the head.)

What was Amy thinking? Did she really intend to tell Joey, "I just killed your wife, so now we can live happily ever after?" Did she think he would be pleased?

The bullet severed Mary Jo's carotid artery, splintered her jaw, and stopped at the base of her brain, an inch away from her spinal column. Miraculously, she survived and was able to describe her assailant. It didn't take long after that, and Amy was picked up by the police on May 22.

By the time the trial started, everybody had changed their stories. Amy insisted that she had no intention of shooting Mary Jo, she just got mad and hit her on the head with the gun, and the gun went off. As for Joey, he swore that he had never been to bed with Amy at all. It was all, he said, a fantasy in her lovely teenage head.

I am shocked—*shocked*—to relate that in order to make her $2 million bail, poor Amy was *forced* to sell the rights to her life story. The result was two books, an off-Broadway play, various newspaper and magazine articles, and three made-for-TV movies, two of which aired opposite each other on the same night, same time slot.

Only Mary Jo, Saint Mary of this unholy trinity, comes off without a trace of sleaze. Despite constant pain and paralysis on the right side of her face, a permanently dislo-cated jaw and deafness in her right ear, she

↜ Little Amy, free at last. After seven years in prison, Amy finally walks free.

managed to forgive Amy, help reduce her sentence, and help win her an early parole in 1999. As for Joey, she always insisted that she believed he'd never touched the girl.

✦✦✦✦ What about Joey? ✦✦✦✦

Joey Buttafuoco did six months in jail for statutory rape and did his best to parlay his fifteen minutes of doubtful fame into a show-biz career. He managed to briefly serve as a cable TV talk show host, and he had a small role in a Sean Connery film. David Letterman discovered that he could get laughs just by saying the name "Buttafuoco" to his television audience. Before the case had even come to trial, and much to the dismay of his lawyer, who'd advised him to keep his lip zipped, Joey phoned in to Howard Stern's radio show and swore he had never had sex with Amy.

Joey had as much trouble keeping his pants zipped. In 1995, he was busted and fined for soliciting an undercover policewoman.

As for Amy, you can find both an official and an unofficial Amy Fisher fan club on the Internet, and guess what? They both have the *same address!* The fan club's news from March 2001 was that Amy was now a mother. She had given birth to a boy, and the father was a fifty-one-year-old man whom Amy had met on the Internet.

✦ Joey Buttafuoco

Acknowledgments

My thanks to Max Allan Collins for calling my attention to Kate Bender, to the LaPorte County Public Library and Historical Society Museum, to Frank Robinson for his great pulpy images of murderous women, to cat and Susie from *Eclipse Comics* for the *True Crime* comic and trading card, to Harley Yee for the wonderfully absurd cover of *Crimes by Women,* to M. Parfitt, intrepid girl journalistic photographer, for the pictures of the house on F Street, and to the guys and gals of Aardvark Books, always a great place to do research.

Recommended Reading

I f you want to find out more about the women in this
book, here's some reading, factual and fictional,
trashy and literate. Some of these books are still in
print; others may be found in your local used bookstore or on the
Internet. And if you can find a copy of *The Bonnie and Clyde Scrapbook*,
consider yourself the luckiest person on Earth. Happy hunting!

Atwood, Margaret. *Alias Grace*. New York: Doubleday, 1996. (Grace
Marks)

Blackburn, Daniel J. *Human Harvest: The Sacramento Murder Story*. New
York: Knightsbridge Publishing Company, 1990. (Dorothea
Puente)

Bravin, Jess. *Squeaky: The Life and Times of Lynette Alice Fromme*. New York: St.
Martin's Press, 1997.

DeMille, Agnes. *Lizzie Borden: A Dance of Death*. Boston: Little, Brown and
Company, 1968.

Eftimiades, Maria. *Lethal Lolita: A True Story of Sex, Scandal and Deadly
Obsession*. New York: St. Martin's Press, 1992. (Amy Fisher)

Fido, Martin. *The Chronicle of Crime: The Infamous Felons of Modern History and
Their Crimes*. New York: Carroll & Graf, 1993.

Geary, Rick. *The Borden Tragedy: A Memoir of the Infamous Double Murder at Fall River Mass, 1892.* New York: NBM Publishing Inc., 1997.

Gelman, B. and Lackman, R. *The Bonnie and Clyde Scrapbook.* New York: Nostalgia Press, n.d. (probably circa 1967).

Hambleton, Ronald. *A Master Killing.* Toronto, Canada: Green Bushell, 1978. (Grace Marks)

Jones, Ann. *Women Who Kill.* New York: Henry Holt and Company, 1980.

Kinney, Madeline G. (revised by Tyler, Gretchen). *The Gunness Story.* La Porte, Indiana: La Porte County Historical Society, 1964, 1984.

McCrumb, Sharyn. *The Ballad of Frankie Silver.* New York: Penguin USA, 1999.

Moodie, Susanna. *Life in the Clearings.* Toronto: The MacMillan Company of Canada Limited, 1959. (Grace Marks)

Norton, Carla. *Disturbed Ground: The True Story of a Diabolical Female Serial Killer.* New York: William Morrow and Company, Inc., 1994. (Dorothea Puente)

Radin, Edward D. *Lizzie Borden: The Untold Story.* New York: Simon and Schuster, 1961.

Sams, Ed. *Lizzie Borden Unlocked.* Ben Lomond, California: Yellow Tulip Press, 2001.

Sheppard, Muriel Earley. *Cabins in the Laurel.* Chapel Hill: University of North Carolina Press, 1935, 1991. (Frankie Silver)

Solanas, Valerie. *SCUM Manifesto.* London: Phoenix Press, 1991.

Symons, Julian. *A Pictorial History of Crime.* New York: Bonanza Books, 1966.

Time Life Books. *Assassination.* Alexandria, Virginia: Time-Warner, 1994.

Trilling, Diana. *Mrs. Harris: The Death of the Scarsdale Diet Doctor.* New York: Harcourt Brace Jovanovich, 1981. (Jean Harris)

Vilar, Irene. *A Message from God in the Atomic Age.* New York: Pantheon Books, 1996. (Lolita Lebron)

Watkins, Maurine. *Chicago.* Carbondale, Illinois: Southern Illinois University Press, 1997. (Beulah May Annan)

Young, Perry Deane. *The Untold Story of Frankie Silver.* Asheboro, North Carolina: Down Home Press, 1998.

And on the Internet:
The Crime Library (http://www.crimelibrary.com) features stories on some of the women in this book and other tender and not-so-tender murderers.

Permissions

Art permissions and credits: pg ii illustration ©1975, Becky Wilson; pg 14 Chicago Historical Society; pg 37 art ©1993, Mark Miraglia and Dan Schaefer; pg 39 art ©1992, Paul Lee; pg 47 The LaPorte Country Historical Society; pg 53 Collections of the New York Public Library; pg 62 Archive photos; pg 67 AP/ Wide World Photos; pg 79 Archive photos; pg 90 Archive photos; pg 114 photo courtesy of Penny Arcade; pg 119 James Smith Noel Collection at Louisiana State University; pg 148 courtesy of Rick Geary, ©1997; pg 151 AP/Wide World photos; pg 153 photo courtesy of Jose B. Riveran, East Harlem Online; pg 155 photo by Jose R. Bas, used by permission of Jose R. Bas; pg 164 Trina Robbins, ©1995; pg 169 photo courtesy of Sacramento Bee; pg 181 Archive photos; pg 182 Archive photos.

An exhaustive effort has been made to clear all photographic permissions for this book. If any required acknowledgments have been omitted, it is unintentional. If notified, the publishers will be pleased to rectify any omission in future editions.

About the Author

TRINA ROBBINS has already written about dark'n'nasty goddesses of the Kali and Lilith persuasion in *Eternally Bad.* She apologizes for her fascination with the dark side—a fascination she shares with countless other women—and promises that once she gets this book out of her system, she'll become nice and maybe even start growing roses.

BOOKS BY TRINA ROBBINS

Eternally Bad

From Girls to Grrrlz

Tomorrow's Heirlooms

The Great Women Superheroes

A Century of Women Cartoonists

Castswalk

Women and the Comics (with Catherine Yronwode)

To Our Readers

CONARI PRESS publishes books on topics ranging from spirituality, personal growth, and relationships to women's issues, parenting, and social issues. Our mission is to publish quality books that will make a difference in people's lives—how we feel about ourselves and how we relate to one another. We value integrity, compassion, and receptivity, both in the books we publish and in the way we do business.

Our readers are our most important resource, and we value your input, suggestions, and ideas about what you would like to see published. Please feel free to contact us, to request our latest book catalog, or to be added to our mailing list.

CONARI PRESS

An imprint of Red Wheel/Weiser, LLC

P.O. Box 612

York Beach, ME 03910-0612

800-423-7087

www.conari.com